Listening & Notetaking Skills

Patricia A. Dunkel & Frank Pialorsi

With

Lynn Bonesteel
Miriam Espeseth
Daphne Mackey
Catherine Mazur-Jefferies

NATIONAL GEOGRAPHIC LEARNING | HEINLE CENGAGE Learning

Australia • Brazil • Japan • Korea • Mexico • Singapore • Spain • United Kingdom • United States

NATIONAL GEOGRAPHIC LEARNING | HEINLE CENGAGE Learning

Listening and Notetaking Skills 3: Advanced Listening Comprehension, Fourth Edition

Patricia A. Dunkel and Frank Pialorsi

Publisher: Sherrise Roehr

Executive Editor: Laura Le Dréan

Director of Global Marketing: Ian Martin

International Marketing Manager: Caitlin Thomas

Product Manager: Emily Stewart

Director, Content and Media Production: Michael Burggren

Content Project Manager: Andrea Bobotas

Print Buyer: Mary Beth Hennebury

Cover Designers: Christopher Roy and Michael Rosenquest

Cover Image: Bruno De Hogues/Getty Images

Compositor: Page Designs International

Student Book ISBN: 978-1-133-95057-8

National Geographic Learning
20 Channel Center Street
Boston, MA 02210
USA

Cengage Learning is a leading provider of customized learning solutions with office locations around the globe, including Singapore, the United Kingdom, Australia, Mexico, Brazil and Japan.

Cengage Learning products are represented in Canada by Nelson Education, Ltd.

Visit National Geographic Learning online at **ngl.cengage.com**

Visit our corporate website at **www.cengage.com**

Printed in the United States of America
1 2 3 4 5 6 7 8 9 10   15 14 13

CONTENTS

Scope and Sequence iv

Unit Walkthrough vi

UNIT 1 **Anthropology:** The Study of Humans and Their Creations 1

Chapter 1 **Anthropologists:** Working in a Diverse Profession 2

Chapter 2 **The Concept of Culture:** Understanding One Another 11

Video **The Gift of Traveling** 20

UNIT 2 **History:** The Passing of Time and Civilizations 23

Chapter 3 **The Egyptian Pyramids:** Houses of Eternity 24

Chapter 4 **The First Emperor of China:** Building an Empire and a House of Eternity 33

Video **Palenque** 42

UNIT 3 **Sociology:** The Changing World of Work 45

Chapter 5 **The Distributed Workforce:** Where and When People Work 46

Chapter 6 **Age and Work:** The Graying of the Workforce 55

Video **An Actor and a Travel Writer** 64

UNIT 4 **Communication:** The Influence of Language, Culture, and Gender 67

Chapter 7 **Classroom Communication:** Language and Culture in the Classroom 68

Chapter 8 **Gender and Communication:** Male–Female Conversation as Cross-cultural Communication 77

Video **Digital Nomad** 86

UNIT 5 **Biology:** From Genetics to Genetic Engineering 89

Chapter 9 **The Origins of Genetics:** Mendel and the Garden Pea Experiment 90

Chapter 10 **Genetic Engineering:** Playing Roulette with Mother Nature's Designs? 99

Video **The Human Journey** 108

Appendix A Audioscripts 111

Appendix B Videoscripts 143

Credits 147

SCOPE AND SEQUENCE

Unit | **Chapter**

1 Anthropology
The Study of Humans and Their Creations

- **1 Anthropologists**
  Working in a Diverse Profession
- **2 The Concept of Culture**
  Understanding One Another

2 History
The Passing of Time and Civilizations

- **3 The Egyptian Pyramids**
  Houses of Eternity
- **4 The First Emperor of China**
  Building an Empire and a House of Eternity

3 Sociology
The Changing World of Work

- **5 The Distributed Workforce**
  Where and When People Work
- **6 Age and Work**
  The Graying of the Workforce

4 Communication
The Influence of Language, Culture, and Gender

- **7 Classroom Communication**
  Language and Culture in the Classroom
- **8 Gender and Communication**
  Male–Female Conversation as Cross-cultural Communication

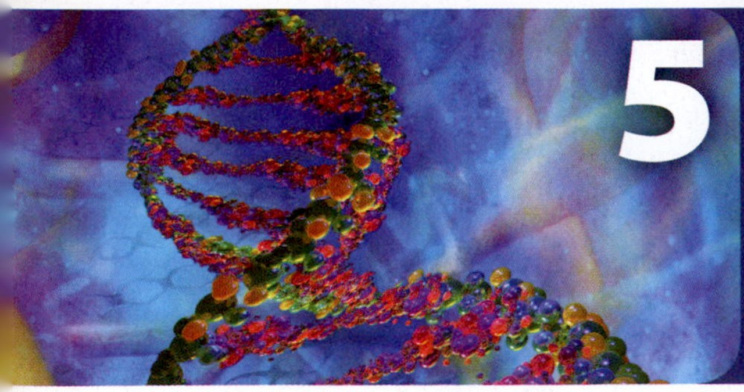

5 Biology
From Genetics to Genetic Engineering

- **9 The Origins of Genetics**
  Mendel and the Garden Pea Experiment
- **10 Genetic Engineering**
  Playing Roulette with Mother Nature's Designs?

Notetaking Preparation	Expansion	Unit Video
• Recording Important Information	**Reading:** Vikings Filed Their Teeth, Skeleton Study Shows	
• Recording Information as a List	**Reading:** Last of the Cave People	
• Recording Numbers and Dates in Notes	**Reading:** Ramses the Great	
• Using Indentation and Spacing Effectively in Notes	**Reading:** Terra-Cotta Army Protects First Emperor's Tomb	
• Using Intonation to Identify New Main Points	**Reading:** "Second Life," Other Virtual Worlds Reshaping Human Interaction	
• Showing Cause and Effect	**Reading:** Why Are Young, Educated Americans Going Back to the Farm?	
• Recording Rhetorical Questions	**Reading:** Love that Lingua Franca	
• Contrast Cues and Charts	**Reading:** Smarter Teams Are More Sensitive, Have More Women?	
• Anticipating and Recording Examples	**Reading:** Genes and Population Genetics	
• Vocabulary: Recovering Meaning as You Listen	**Reading:** Food: How Altered?	

UNIT WALKTHROUGH

New to This Edition

- Authentic **National Geographic videos** provide a meaningful context for discussion and application of essential listening, notetaking, and vocabulary skills.
- New and updated **academic lectures** offer compelling, cross-curricular content that simulate authentic scenarios for maximum academic readiness.
- Every unit introduces a focused aspect of **notetaking** and provides varied opportunities for practice and application of the skill.

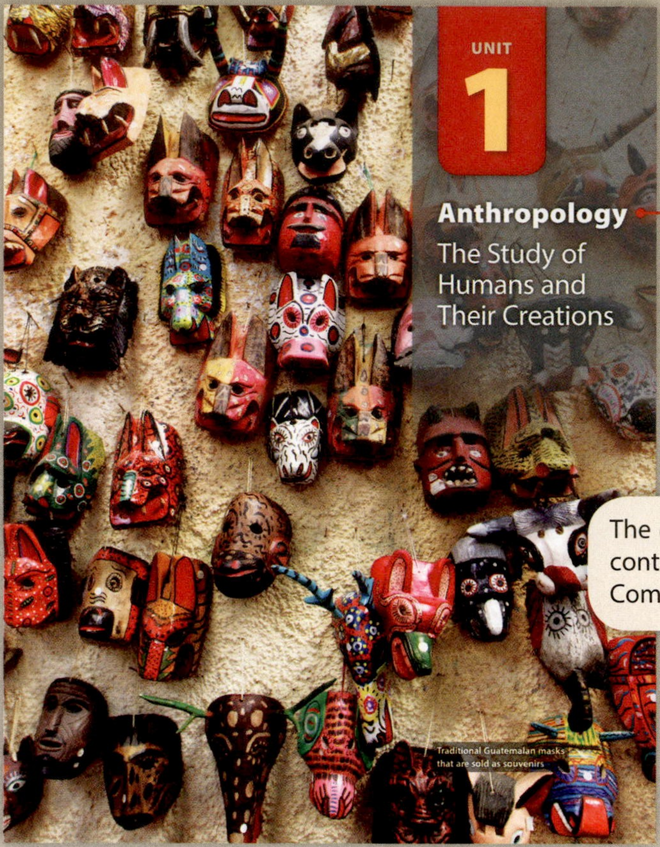

The *Unit Theme* focuses on an academic content area relevant to students' lives such as Communication, Biology, and Anthropology.

Before Listening activities prepare students for success by activating background knowledge and providing the language and skills necessary for comprehension.

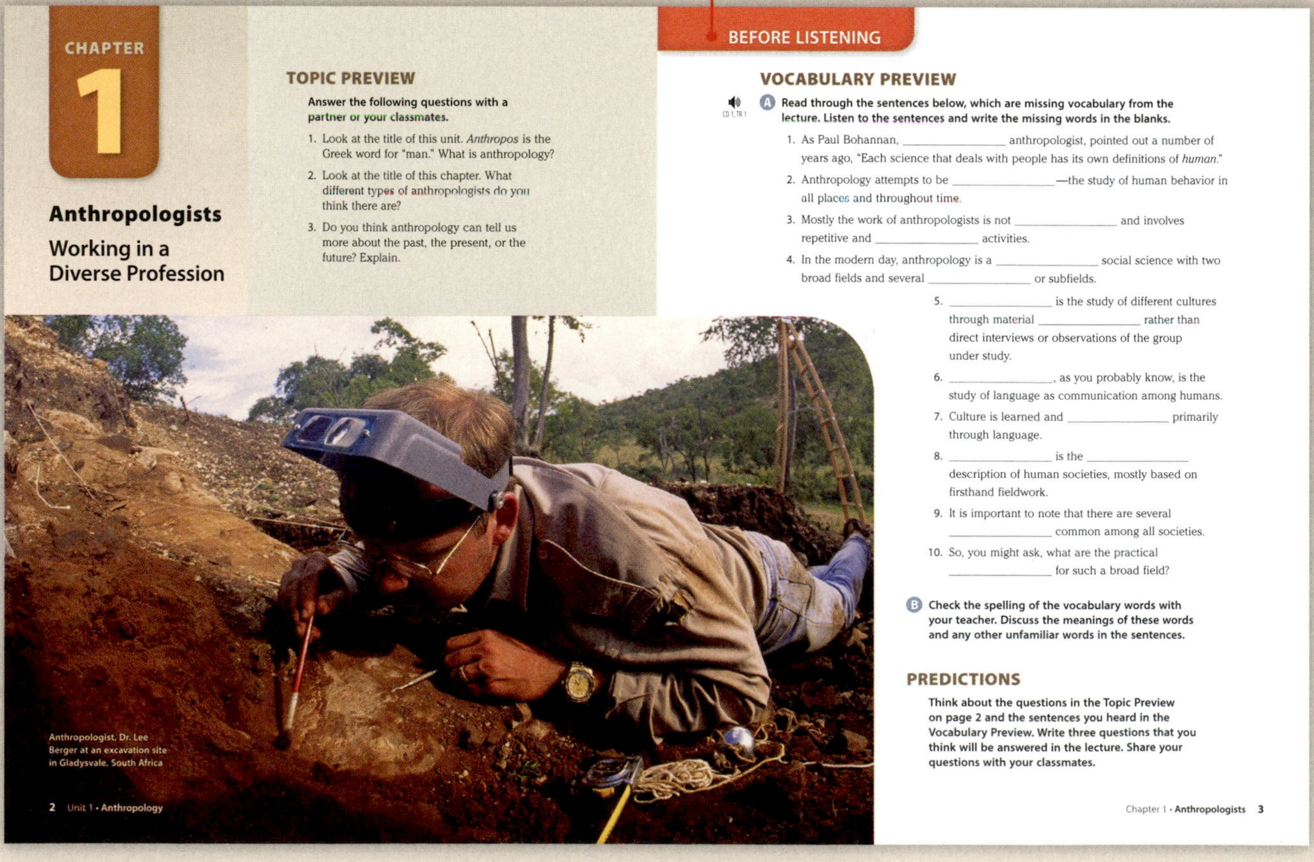

CHAPTER 1

Anthropologists

Working in a Diverse Profession

TOPIC PREVIEW

Answer the following questions with a partner or your classmates.

1. Look at the title of this unit. *Anthropos* is the Greek word for "man." What is anthropology?
2. Look at the title of this chapter. What different types of anthropologists do you think there are?
3. Do you think anthropology can tell us more about the past, the present, or the future? Explain.

Anthropologist, Dr. Lee Berger at an excavation site in Gladysvale, South Africa

2 Unit 1 • Anthropology

BEFORE LISTENING

VOCABULARY PREVIEW

CD 1, TR 1

A Read through the sentences below, which are missing vocabulary from the lecture. Listen to the sentences and write the missing words in the blanks.

1. As Paul Bohannan, ________ anthropologist, pointed out a number of years ago, "Each science that deals with people has its own definitions of *human*."
2. Anthropology attempts to be ________—the study of human behavior in all places and throughout time.
3. Mostly the work of anthropologists is not ________ and involves repetitive and ________ activities.
4. In the modern day, anthropology is a ________ social science with two broad fields and several ________ or subfields.
5. ________ is the study of different cultures through material ________ rather than direct interviews or observations of the group under study.
6. ________, as you probably know, is the study of language as communication among humans.
7. Culture is learned and ________ primarily through language.
8. ________ is the ________ description of human societies, mostly based on firsthand fieldwork.
9. It is important to note that there are several ________ common among all societies.
10. So, you might ask, what are the practical ________ for such a broad field?

B Check the spelling of the vocabulary words with your teacher. Discuss the meanings of these words and any other unfamiliar words in the sentences.

PREDICTIONS

Think about the questions in the Topic Preview on page 2 and the sentences you heard in the Vocabulary Preview. Write three questions that you think will be answered in the lecture. Share your questions with your classmates.

Chapter 1 • Anthropologists 3

The *Notetaking Preparation* section presents a variety of effective notetaking techniques. Using content from the unit, students practice these techniques in authentic academic situations.

NOTETAKING PREPARATION

Recording Important Information

Efficient notetakers do not write down every word of a lecture. Here are some tips for taking notes:

- Listen for and note the main ideas of the lecture.
- Write only the key words, not complete sentences.
- Use abbreviations for common words or for a specific word that you hear many times in the lecture. There are many ways to abbreviate. Figure out what abbreviations make sense to you. Here are some examples:

  shorten long words to one or two syllables
  problem = *prob* anthropology = *anthro*

  leave out the vowels
  problem = *prb* or *prblm*

  use a single letter for a high-frequency word
  Egypt = *E* price = *p*

- When you miss something in the lecture, leave some space.
- After a lecture, go back and write out any words you abbreviated and might not remember later. Check with the lecturer or another student to fill in information you missed.

A Look at the abbreviations. Match the abbreviations to words from the lecture.

1. *devt*	____ cultural	6. *anthro*	____ evolution
2. *comp*	____ anatomy	7. *phys*	____ analysis
3. *anat*	____ development	8. *As*	____ physical
4. *cult*	____ subjects	9. *evol*	____ anthropologists
5. *subj*	____ comparative	10. *anlys*	____ anthropology

B Listen to sentences from the lecture. Take notes. Use abbreviations where possible.

1. ____
2. ____
3. ____
4. ____
5. ____

4 Unit 1 • Anthropology

Notetaking Skills

Throughout the *Listening & Notetaking Skills* series, learners develop a wide variety of notetaking strategies necessary for academic success. Learners are taught the essential principles of notetaking and encouraged to personalize the strategies for maximum results.

Listening sections introduce the academic lecture. Learners listen to the lecture three times, focusing on a different listening and notetaking skill with each repetition.

LISTENING

FIRST LISTENING

Listen to the lecture and number the slides on this page and the next in the order they would be shown during the lecture. Write the number of the slide on the line provided and answer the question to the right of the slide.

Coexistence of Culture and Society

Isolated cultures

Multicultural or pluralist

Subcultures

Slide # ____

What is an example of a pluralist society?

____

A Particular Culture

A shared way of life
- Ways of thinking, acting, feeling
- Concrete things

Slide # ____

What are some concrete things that tell us about a particular culture?

____

Similarities Across Cultures

Importance of discovering similarities

Universals among societies

The role of the individual

Slide # ____

How many "universals" among all cultures does the lecturer mention?

____

Cultural Anthropology

Why study cultural anthropology?
- Fascinating story of cultural growth
- Learn and use a foreign language
- Intercultural understanding

Slide # ____

What is the definition of cultural anthropology?

____

What Is Culture?

Murdock / Tylor / Kessing

Learned, socially transmitted behavior

Slide # ____

How many categories did Murdock list?

____

14 Unit 1 • Anthropology

Chapter 2 • The Concept of Culture 15

After Listening sections provide learners with opportunities to discuss the lecture through pair and group activities.

AFTER LISTENING

ACCURACY CHECK

CD 1, TR 12

You will hear questions about the lecture. Answer each question by referring to the notes that you took while listening to the lecture.

1. a. Mead
   b. Tylor
   c. Murdock
2. a. savagery
   b. language
   c. barbarism
3. a. 1962
   b. 1989
   c. 1993
4. a. communication
   b. social variables
   c. empathy and curiosity
5. a. a remote tribe
   b. a pluralistic society
   c. people in a large city
6. a. civilization
   b. savagery
   c. multiculturalism
7. a. political
   b. military
   c. informal
8. a. Seelye
   b. Sapir
   c. Benedict

The *Oral Summary* asks learners to use their notes to reconstruct the content of the lecture.

ORAL SUMMARY

Use your notes to create an oral summary of the lecture with a partner. As you work together, add details to your notes that your partner included but you had missed.

DISCUSSION

Discuss the following questions with a classmate or in a small group.

1. After listening to the lecture, do you find *culture* difficult or easy to define? What is your definition? In what ways is it the same or different from definitions in the lecture?
2. List four or five cultural "generalizations" that foreigners may have about your country.
3. "If a group or society is small, isolated, and stable, it might also share a single culture." Do you know of any such "single" cultures in the world? What would you look for to decide if a group of people share a "single" culture?

Chapter 2 • The Concept of Culture 17

An *Expansion* section in each chapter includes high-interest National Geographic articles that present information related to the unit theme.

Through guided prompts, *Discussion* activities provide opportunities for learners to hone communicative and critical thinking skills.

EXPANSION

PRE-READING

The following Reading is about the experiences of an anthropological research team in the mountains of Papua New Guinea. Before you read, answer the following questions. Share your answers with a classmate.

1. Look at the title of the article and the photograph on the next page. Write two things that you expect to learn about the "Cave People" from the article.
2. In the lecture, the speaker discussed reasons to study cultural anthropology. Why would a team of researchers want to visit these people in Papua New Guinea?

READING

Now read the article.

Last of the Cave People

by Mark Jenkins

The vast geographic variation of Papua New Guinea created tremendous biological diversity, which in turn was accompanied by enormous cultural diversity. It is only in the most deeply inaccessible regions that enclaves of traditionally nomadic people, like the Meakambut, still exist. The Meakambut were unknown to the outside world until the 1960s. In 1991 anthropologist Borut Telban spent a week in the area and found only 11 Meakambut. When Telban returned in 2001, he couldn't locate them again.

In hopes of meeting up with these last seminomadic holdouts, an anthropological researcher named Nancy Sullivan sent out a team to find the Meakambut and inventory their caves. Sullivan's team discovered 52 surviving Meakambut and 105 caves with names.

Our team flies into the Sepik River basin. We skim up smaller and smaller tributaries in a motor dugout. Finally we strike out on foot into the mountains. We try reaching the Meakambut by jungle telephone: Three men pound the trunk of a towering tree with wooden bats. When this doesn't work, we set out on a two-day trek to the group's last known whereabouts.

At noon the next day, two Meakambut men come striding into our camp. They recognize Joshua Meraveka, a member of Sullivan's team. He introduces them as John and Mark Aiyo. John is a leader of the Meakambut. While waiting there for the rest of the Embarakal to arrive, John explains cave life to me. He says they like their hunter-gatherer life and have no interest in changing it.

Before long, the rest of the Meakambut arrive. This is when we first encounter Lidia, curled up by the fire, coughing horribly. A member of our team, an emergency medical technician, examines Lidia. He determines that she likely has a life-threatening case of pneumonia and gives her double doses of antibiotics and Tylenol. We suggest that first thing in the morning she be carried out of the mountains, to a clinic in the village of Amboin. Two other Meakambut are also seriously ill.

One man from our team, Sebastian Haraha, is an ethnographer who has come to pinpoint the locations of the Meakambut's caves. He hopes to register them so the homeland of the Meakambut will be protected. Now, he volunteers to escort the sick.

Two nights later, John begins to let down his guard. He admits that his group hasn't eaten meat or killed a pig for over three months. He is deeply worried for his people. When the campfire dies out, John whispers something he wants me to pass on to the government of Papua New Guinea.

The next morning our team leaves the mountains. We reach our motor dugout and travel downstream

18 Unit 1 • Anthropology

A member of the Meakambut tribe wearing bird-feather headdress

to the village of Awim and learn that Lidia and the others are here. Lidia is alive. Simple antibiotics have saved her.

At breakfast, I find Sebastian Haraha. "Protecting the caves? What does it matter if there are no Meakambut left?" asks Sebastian. "The Meakambut are on the edge of extinction. They are dying from easily treatable illnesses. In ten years they could be completely gone, and their culture and language would vanish. When I get back to Port Moresby, I'm going to walk straight into the prime minister's office and do something."

I nod and pass along John's message: "We, the Meakambut people, will give up hunting and always moving and living in the mountain caves if the government will give us a health clinic and a school, and two shovels and two axes, so we can build homes."

The Meakambut continue to live without access to government services. But they have partly settled in homes on the ridgetop camp of Tembakapa. Despite the threat of encroachment by miners, they continue to hunt and gather on their traditional land.

DISCUSSION

Discuss these questions with a classmate.

1. What surprised or interested you most about the culture described in the passage? Why?
2. What was the role of the anthropologists in this story? How was it similar to or different from what you learned about anthropologists and ethnologists in the lecture?
3. What information from the lecture was exemplified in the article?

RESEARCH PROJECT

Individually or in a group, research one of the following topics. Write a short paper on the topic, or plan and present a group presentation to inform the class about the topic.

1. Isolated cultures: Where do they still exist, and what challenges do they face?
2. Research in cultural anthropology: What similarities and differences exist between your culture and another?
3. Intercultural understanding: Does studying or living in another culture change an individual's values? Provide evidence to support your opinion.
4. Another related topic that interests you or your group.

Chapter 2 • The Concept of Culture 19

Additional expansion activities centered on the unit theme include online research, short essays, and classroom presentations for academic preparation.

Unit Video

Each unit ends with an authentic **National Geographic** video that is related to the unit theme. Most of the videos are in a lecture format, giving students a further opportunity to practice notetaking skills.

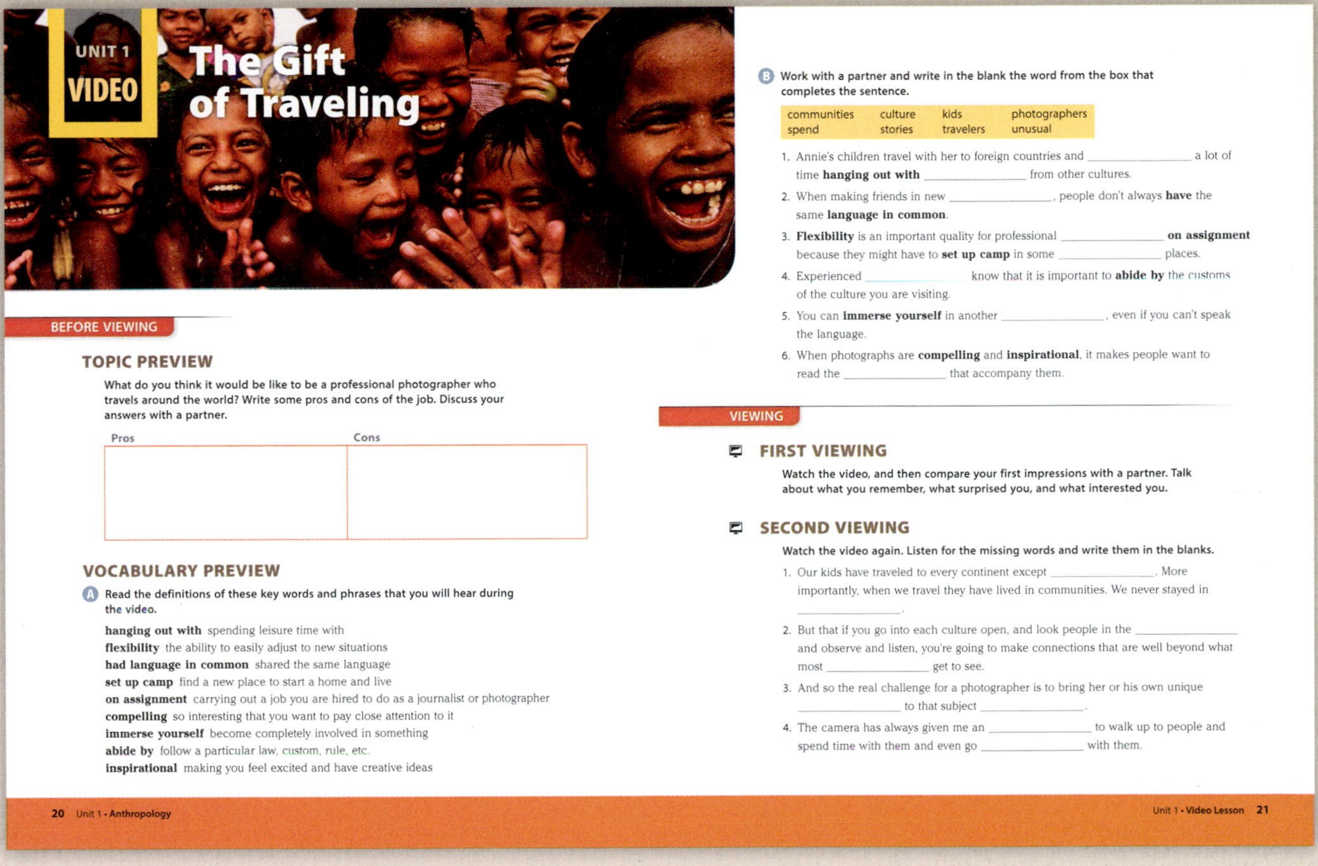
UNIT 1 VIDEO

The Gift of Traveling

BEFORE VIEWING

TOPIC PREVIEW

What do you think it would be like to be a professional photographer who travels around the world? Write some pros and cons of the job. Discuss your answers with a partner.

Pros	Cons

VOCABULARY PREVIEW

A Read the definitions of these key words and phrases that you will hear during the video.

hanging out with spending leisure time with
flexibility the ability to easily adjust to new situations
had language in common shared the same language
set up camp find a new place to start a home and live
on assignment carrying out a job you are hired to do as a journalist or photographer
compelling so interesting that you want to pay close attention to it
immerse yourself become completely involved in something
abide by follow a particular law, custom, rule, etc.
inspirational making you feel excited and have creative ideas

B Work with a partner and write in the blank the word from the box that completes the sentence.

communities	culture	kids	photographers
spend	stories	travelers	unusual

1. Annie's children travel with her to foreign countries and ______ a lot of time **hanging out with** ______ from other cultures.
2. When making friends in new ______, people don't always **have** the same **language in common**.
3. **Flexibility** is an important quality for professional ______ **on assignment** because they might have to **set up camp** in some ______ places.
4. Experienced ______ know that it is important to **abide by** the customs of the culture you are visiting.
5. You can **immerse yourself** in another ______, even if you can't speak the language.
6. When photographs are **compelling** and **inspirational**, it makes people want to read the ______ that accompany them.

VIEWING

FIRST VIEWING

Watch the video, and then compare your first impressions with a partner. Talk about what you remember, what surprised you, and what interested you.

SECOND VIEWING

Watch the video again. Listen for the missing words and write them in the blanks.

1. Our kids have traveled to every continent except ______. More importantly, when we travel they have lived in communities. We never stayed in ______.
2. But that if you go into each culture open, and look people in the ______ and observe and listen, you're going to make connections that are well beyond what most ______ get to see.
3. And so the real challenge for a photographer is to bring her or his own unique ______ to that subject ______.
4. The camera has always given me an ______ to walk up to people and spend time with them and even go ______ with them.

20 Unit 1 • Anthropology

Unit 1 • Video Lesson 21

Listening and Notetaking Skills Series Components

The Audio CDs provide all the lectures and listening activities contained in the Student Book.

The Video DVD contains five authentic **National Geographic** videos relating to the units in the book.

UNIT 1

Anthropology

The Study of Humans and Their Creations

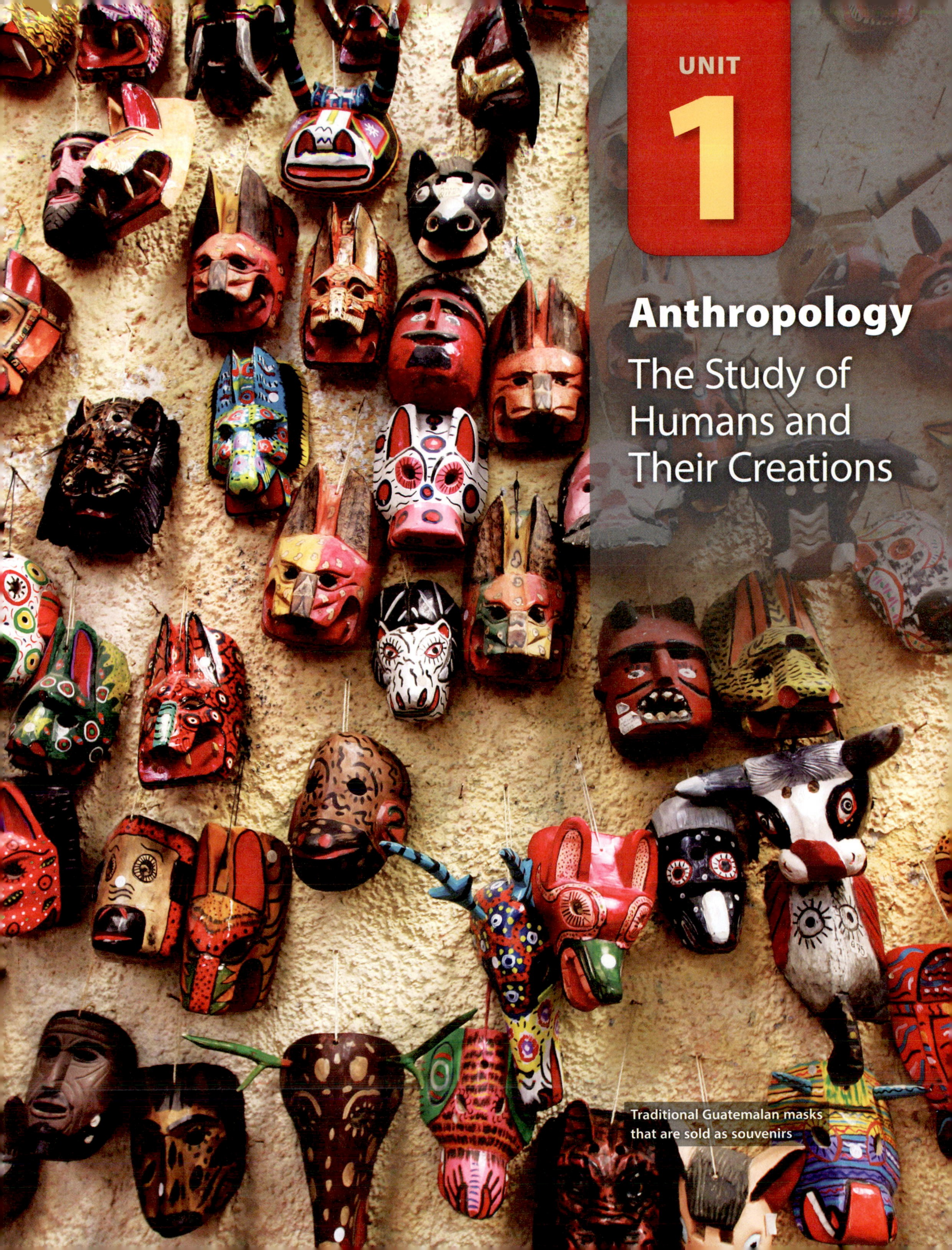

Traditional Guatemalan masks that are sold as souvenirs

CHAPTER

1

Anthropologists

Working in a Diverse Profession

TOPIC PREVIEW

Answer the following questions with a partner or your classmates.

1. Look at the title of this unit. *Anthropos* is the Greek word for "man." What is anthropology?
2. Look at the title of this chapter. What different types of anthropologists do you think there are?
3. Do you think anthropology can tell us more about the past, the present, or the future? Explain.

Anthropologist Dr. Lee Berger at an excavation site in Gladysvale, South Africa

VOCABULARY PREVIEW

CD 1, TR 1

A Read through the sentences below, which are missing vocabulary from the lecture. Listen to the sentences and write the missing words in the blanks.

1. As Paul Bohannan, ________________ anthropologist, pointed out a number of years ago, "Each science that deals with people has its own definitions of *human*."
2. Anthropology attempts to be ________________—the study of human behavior in all places and throughout time.
3. Mostly the work of anthropologists is not ________________ and involves repetitive and ________________ activities.
4. In the modern day, anthropology is a ________________ social science with two broad fields and several ________________ or subfields.
5. ________________ is the study of different cultures through material ________________ rather than direct interviews or observations of the group under study.
6. ________________, as you probably know, is the study of language as communication among humans.
7. Culture is learned and ________________ primarily through language.
8. ________________ is the ________________ description of human societies, mostly based on firsthand fieldwork.
9. It is important to note that there are several ________________ common among all societies.
10. So, you might ask, what are the practical ________________ for such a broad field?

B Check the spelling of the vocabulary words with your teacher. Discuss the meanings of these words and any other unfamiliar words in the sentences.

PREDICTIONS

Think about the questions in the Topic Preview on page 2 and the sentences you heard in the Vocabulary Preview. Write three questions that you think will be answered in the lecture. Share your questions with your classmates.

NOTETAKING PREPARATION

Recording Important Information

Efficient notetakers do not write down every word of a lecture. Here are some tips for taking notes:

- Listen for and note the main ideas of the lecture.
- Write only the key words, not complete sentences.
- Use abbreviations for common words or for a specific word that you hear many times in the lecture. There are many ways to abbreviate. Figure out what abbreviations make sense to you. Here are some examples:

  shorten long words to one or two syllables
  problem = *prob*   anthropology = *anthro*

  leave out the vowels
  problem = *prb* or *prblm*

  use a single letter for a high-frequency word
  Egypt = *E*   price = *p*

- When you miss something in the lecture, leave some space.
- After a lecture, go back and write out any words you abbreviated and might not remember later. Check with the lecturer or another student to fill in information you missed.

A **Look at the abbreviations. Match the abbreviations to words from the lecture.**

1. *devt*	____ cultural	6. *anthro*	____ evolution
2. *comp*	____ anatomy	7. *phys*	____ analysis
3. *anat*	____ development	8. *As*	____ physical
4. *cult*	____ subjects	9. *evol*	____ anthropologists
5. *subj*	____ comparative	10. *anlys*	____ anthropology

CD 1, TR 2

B **Listen to sentences from the lecture. Take notes. Use abbreviations where possible.**

1. ______________________________
2. ______________________________
3. ______________________________
4. ______________________________
5. ______________________________

FIRST LISTENING

CD 1, TR 3

Listen to the lecture and number the slides on this page and the next in the order they would be shown during the lecture. Write the number of the slide on the line provided and answer the question to the right of the slide.

Subfields of Cultural Anthropology

Archaeology

Linguistics

Ethnography

Psychological anthropology

Slide #_____

What is ethnography?

Universals in All Societies

Anthropology today

- Applied anthropology

Slide #_____

Are anthropologists only interested in the past?

Physical Anthropology

Definition

Related subjects

Ways to study evolution of humans

Slide #_____

What is *physical anthropology*?

What Is Anthropology?

Literal definition

Misconceptions

My definition

Development of anthropology

Slide #_____

What is the lecture going to explain?

Cultural Anthropology

Definition

Study of specific locations or groups

- Margaret Mead
- Clyde Kluckhohn

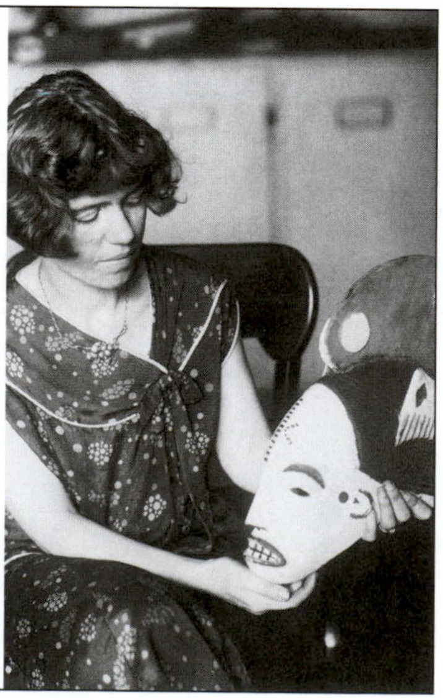

Slide #_____

What is *cultural anthropology*?

SECOND LISTENING

CD 1, TR 4

Now that you've listened to the lecture once, listen to it again and take notes. Write on a separate piece of paper.

THIRD LISTENING

CD 1, TR 5

You will hear parts of the lecture again. Look through your notes as you listen. A notetaking mentor will discuss the notes. Circle the answer that is closest to the notes you took, and put a check (✓) next to the notes that the mentor wrote.

Part 1

1. a.
cult anthro = lrnd behav in hum soc

b.
cultural anthropology = study learned behavior human societies

2. a.
geog areas
- Mead = Samoa
- SW US

b.
geog areas
- Mead = Samoa
- (Cluckho ??) = SW US

c.
geog areas
- Mead = Samoa
- Kluckhohn = SW US

Part 2

3. a.
cult anthro – arch – ling – ethno

b.
cult anthro & sci study hum cult disc in next lecture

c.
cult anthro subfields:
- arch, ling, ethno

Part 3

4. a.
arch = diff cult – not int, obs
ex – King Tut 1922

b.
arch = study of diff'ent cults thru mat srces
≠ int'vws + obs'ns
- ex: Tut's tomb 1922

c.
archaeol'gy is the stud of diff cult's through material sources rather than dir interviews or obs of the grp under study
1 ex – famous arch site disc past cent was K Tut's tomb near (??) Egypt in 1922

ACCURACY CHECK

CD 1, TR 6

You will hear questions about the lecture. Answer each question by referring to the notes that you took while listening to the lecture.

1. a. man
   b. the study of man
   c. a choice-making animal
2. a. history
   b. describing societies
   c. the ideal society
3. a. the Navajo
   b. the Americas
   c. Samoa and New Guinea
4. a. cultural anthropology
   b. physical anthropology
   c. psychological anthropology
5. a. *Mirror for Man*
   b. study of Navajo Indians
   c. research in Samoa and New Guinea
6. a. sociology
   b. ethnology
   c. archaeology
7. a. a universal
   b. skills and attitudes
   c. practical applications of anthropology
8. a. teaching
   b. urban planning
   c. museum administration

ORAL SUMMARY

Use your notes to create an oral summary of the lecture with a partner. As you work together, add details to your notes that your partner included but you had missed.

DISCUSSION

Discuss the following questions with a classmate or in a small group.

1. Anthropology is a very broad field. Where does anthropology end and other fields begin? In other words, what is the difference between anthropology and fields such as history or religion?
2. What was the principal role of the anthropologist in the past and how is that role changing?
3. Can you think of ways that applied anthropology is useful in your community?

EXPANSION

PRE-READING

The following Reading is about an anthropologist's findings. Before you read, answer the following questions. Share your answers with a classmate.

1. Look at the title and headings in the Reading article. Write the name of a subfield of anthropology you expect to learn more about in the article.
2. Using information you learned in the lecture, what are two things you expect to learn about the Vikings from an anthropological study?

READING

Now read the article.

Vikings Filed Their Teeth, Skeleton Study Shows

Contrary to popular belief, the Vikings took great pride in their looks. One beautification technique of the ancient Norsemen was to file their teeth. A Swedish anthropologist analyzed 557 Viking skeletons dating from AD 800 to 1050 and discovered that 24 of them bore deep, horizontal grooves across their upper front teeth. It's the first time that dental modification—a practice found in cultures around the world—has been seen in human skeletons from Europe.

"These unique finds of deliberate dental modification . . . reveal what we did not know before, that this custom is practiced around the world and also in Europe," said Caroline Arcini, an anthropologist at the National Heritage Board in Lund, Sweden.

Acquisitive Habits

Researchers say the Vikings may have learned the practice of filing their teeth from a foreign culture. "Vikings are well known for their acquisitive habits, but until now we've thought of this in terms of gold, silver, and booty, not facial decoration," said William Fitzhugh, a Viking expert at the Smithsonian National Museum of Natural History in Washington, D.C.

"Maybe they adopted the idea of mutilating their teeth from people they met on their voyages," Arcini said. "The only place I know of [where people] have similar horizontal filing marks on their teeth . . . is the area of the Great Lakes in North America and the present states of Illinois, Arizona, and Georgia."

Social Identification

People in many cultures have been modifying their teeth for several thousand years. Some of the oldest cases of tooth modification come from Mexico, dating as far back as 1400 BCE. But the Viking discovery is the first historical example of ceremonial dental modification among Europeans.

The skeletons Arcini analyzed were discovered at several Viking-era burial sites in Sweden and

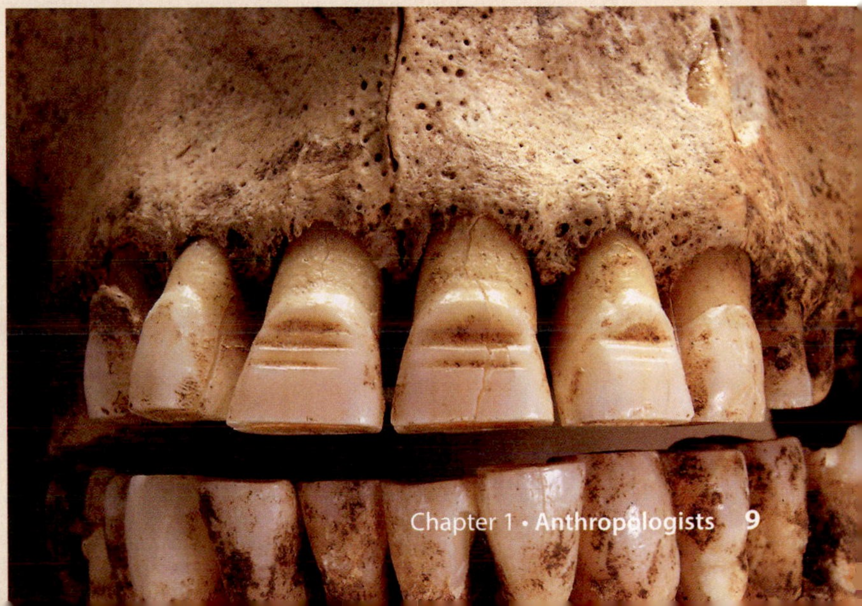

Replica of a Viking wooden church

Denmark. The 24 skeletons she found with filed teeth all belonged to men. The marks were cut deep into the enamel and occurred often in pairs or triplets. "I can conclude that the filed furrows in the front teeth of 24 Viking men are deliberately made and not the result of using the teeth as a tool," Arcini said. She also noted that the marks are so well made that a person of great skill most likely filed them.

Why the Viking men had their teeth modified remains a mystery, but it's likely that the marks represented some kind of achievement. "I think the Vikings' filed furrows should be seen as a social identification," Arcini, the Swedish anthropologist, said. "Maybe they were brave warriors who got a furrow each time they won a battle, or tradesmen who traveled together."

Fitzhugh, of the Smithsonian, says the reasons may have been partly aesthetic. "We do know that the Vikings took pride in their appearance, combed their hair, and ironed their clothes with hot rocks," Fitzhugh said. "They now seem to have taken pain to decorate their teeth."

DISCUSSION

Discuss these questions with a classmate.

1. What surprised or interested you most about the findings described in the passage? Why?
2. How was the information in the reading similar to or different from the information in the lecture?
3. Summarize what you have learned about anthropology and what it can tell us about a people.

RESEARCH PROJECT

Individually or with a partner, find a current article on a discovery that changes how anthropologists think about a people or place. Write up the details for a short presentation to the class.

Be sure to include the following:

- What is the source of your information?
- Under which branch of anthropology does the discovery fall?
- Who sponsored the research or expedition resulting in the finding?
- What are the significant details (who? what? where?) of the finding?

CHAPTER

2

The Concept of Culture

Understanding One Another

TOPIC PREVIEW

Answer the following questions with a partner or your classmates.

1. Look at the title of this chapter. What do we mean by a "concept of culture"? Do you think people have different concepts, or ideas, about what "culture" is?
2. Look at the photograph on this page. What elements of culture does it illustrate?
3. How curious are you about other cultures? Do you know students from other cultures? In what ways, if any, do you seem different?

Ethnic Papua New Guinean in traditional dress at a sing-sing festival

BEFORE LISTENING

VOCABULARY PREVIEW

CD 1, TR 7

A **Read through the sentences below, which are missing vocabulary from the lecture. Listen to the sentences and write the missing words in the blanks.**

1. Culture is that ________________ whole which includes knowledge, belief, art, law, morals, custom, and any other capabilities and habits ________________ by man as a member of society.
2. Another definition of culture that many find useful is "the totality of learned, socially ________________ behavior."
3. Ned Seelye, in his 1993 book *Teaching Culture*, lists six skills to ________________ and support ________________ communication.
4. ________________ curiosity about another culture and ________________ toward its members.
5. Recognize that different roles and other social ________________ such as age, sex, social class, religion, ________________, and place of residence affect the way people speak and behave.
6. Realize that effective communication requires discovering the culturally ________________ images of people when they think, act, and react to the world around them.
7. Recognize that ________________ variables and ________________ shape people's behavior in important ways.
8. Understand that people generally act the way they do because they are ________________ the options their society allows for ________________ basic physical and psychological needs.
9. Culture and society must ________________.
10. In the long history of human life, ________________ is a fairly recent ________________.

B **Check the spelling of the vocabulary words with your teacher. Discuss the meanings of these words and any other unfamiliar words in the sentences.**

PREDICTIONS

Think about the questions in the Topic Preview on page 11 and the sentences you heard in the Vocabulary Preview. Write three questions that you think will be answered in the lecture. Share your questions with your classmates.

NOTETAKING PREPARATION

Recording Information as a List

Listen for cues that show a lecturer is going to list information. Use a heading and numbers, letters, or bullets to show the information clearly. Here are some examples.

Cues to listen for	Notes
The report gave two reasons for the failure First, . . . Then, . . .	Why fail – 1. 2.
Let me give you some examples of this type of problem One is . . . Another . . . The last . . . Finally, . . .	Ex of prob • • • •

A **Look at the notes below and answer the questions.**

1. Who do you think Benedict, Tylor, and Morgan are?
2. What do you think the following abbreviations stand for?
   a. hum'ty b. stgs c. civiliz d. for. lang
3. How many answers are given to the question at the beginning of the notes?

Why stdy cult anthro? Benedict says stry hum'ty fasc (Tylor & Morgan – cult devt = 3 stgs – savg'ry, barb'ism, civiliz) lrn & use for. lang

CD 1, TR 8

B **Listen to part of the lecture for the notes in A above. Then rewrite the notes in the space below to show the information in lists.**

FIRST LISTENING

CD 1, TR 9

Listen to the lecture and number the slides on this page and the next in the order they would be shown during the lecture. Write the number of the slide on the line provided and answer the question to the right of the slide.

Coexistence of Culture and Society

Isolated cultures

Multicultural or pluralist

Subcultures

Slide #_____

What is an example of a pluralist society?

A Particular Culture

A shared way of life

- Ways of thinking, acting, feeling
- Concrete things

Slide #_____

What are some concrete things that tell us about a particular culture?

Similarities Across Cultures

Importance of discovering similarities

Universals among societies

The role of the individual

Slide #_____

How many "universals" among all cultures does the lecturer mention?

Cultural Anthropology

Why study cultural anthropology?

- Fascinating story of cultural growth
- Learn and use a foreign language
- Intercultural understanding

Slide #_____

What is the definition of cultural anthropology?

What Is Culture?

Murdock / Tylor / Kessing

Learned, socially transmitted behavior

Slide #_____

How many categories did Murdock list?

SECOND LISTENING

CD 1, TR 10

Now that you've listened to the lecture once, listen to it again and take notes. Write on a separate piece of paper.

THIRD LISTENING

CD 1, TR 11

You will hear parts of the lecture again. Look through your notes as you listen. A notetaking mentor will discuss the notes. Circle the answer that is closest to the notes you took, and put a check (✓) next to the notes that the mentor wrote.

Part 1

1. a.

Cult anthro = study of cult, liv & dead. In total includes ling, arch, ethnology

b.

Cult anthro = st. of cult (liv & dead)
- ling = study spch frms
- arch = " dead cult
- ethno = " liv cult (can be obs)

Part 2

2. a.

Teaching Culture – 6 skills
1. cult curiosty
2. rec roles aff spk & beh
3. rlize eff comm req disc cult-cond'd imgs
4. rec sit'l var shap beh
5. und. ppl act bec ex opt'ns to sat phys & psych nds
6. dev ablty to eval gen'ztion & loc/org info

b.

Sealy (sp??) – skills for intc'l comm
1. curiosty & emp
2. rec roles aff spk & beh
3. rlize eff comm req disc cult-cond'd imgs
4. rec sit'l var shap beh
5. und ppl act bec ex opt'ns to sat phys & psych nds
6. dev ablty to eval gen'ztion & loc/org info

c.

1. curiosty & emp
2. rec roles aff spk & beh
3. rlize eff comm req disc cult-cond'd imgs
4. rec sit'l var shap beh
5. und. ppl act bec ex opt'ns to sat phys & psych nds
6. dev ablty to eval gen'ztion & loc/org info

Part 3

3. a.

Universals
1. rewards & punishment
2. withhld info fr young
3. contr cult educ yng

b.

Universals of culture – rewds & punshmt – wthhld info – incl faults in ldrs – taboos – educ young for dom pos

c.

Univs'ls
- use rwds & pnish't to enc corr beh.
- wihld info (eg ldrs, taboos)
- ctrl'g cult educ yng to strngthn dom pos

AFTER LISTENING

ACCURACY CHECK

CD 1, TR 12

You will hear questions about the lecture. Answer each question by referring to the notes that you took while listening to the lecture.

1. a. Mead
   b. Tylor
   c. Murdock

2. a. savagery
   b. language
   c. barbarism

3. a. 1962
   b. 1989
   c. 1993

4. a. communication
   b. social variables
   c. empathy and curiosity

5. a. a remote tribe
   b. a pluralistic society
   c. people in a large city

6. a. civilization
   b. savagery
   c. multiculturalism

7. a. political
   b. military
   c. informal

8. a. Seelye
   b. Sapir
   c. Benedict

ORAL SUMMARY

Use your notes to create an oral summary of the lecture with a partner. As you work together, add details to your notes that your partner included but you had missed.

DISCUSSION

Discuss the following questions with a classmate or in a small group.

1. After listening to the lecture, do you find *culture* difficult or easy to define? What is your definition? In what ways is it the same or different from definitions in the lecture?
2. List four or five cultural "generalizations" that foreigners may have about your country.
3. "If a group or society is small, isolated, and stable, it might also share a single culture." Do you know of any such "single" cultures in the world? What would you look for to decide if a group of people share a "single" culture?

PRE-READING

The following Reading is about the experiences of an anthropological research team in the mountains of Papua New Guinea. Before you read, answer the following questions. Share your answers with a classmate.

1. Look at the title of the article and the photograph on the next page. Write two things that you expect to learn about the "Cave People" from the article.
2. In the lecture, the speaker discussed reasons to study cultural anthropology. Why would a team of researchers want to visit these people in Papua New Guinea?

READING

Now read the article.

Last of the Cave People

The vast geographic variation of Papua New Guinea created tremendous biological diversity, which in turn was accompanied by enormous cultural diversity. It is only in the most deeply inaccessible regions that enclaves of traditionally nomadic people, like the Meakambut, still exist. The Meakambut were unknown to the outside world until the 1960s. In 1991 anthropologist Borut Telban spent a week in the area and found only 11 Meakambut. When Telban returned in 2001, he couldn't locate them again.

In hopes of meeting up with these last semi-nomadic holdouts, an anthropological researcher named Nancy Sullivan sent out a team to find the Meakambut and inventory their caves. Sullivan's team discovered 52 surviving Meakambut and 105 caves with names.

Our team flies into the Sepik River basin. We skim up smaller and smaller tributaries in a motor dugout. Finally we strike out on foot into the mountains. We try reaching the Meakambut by jungle telephone: Three men pound the trunk of a towering tree with wooden bats. When this doesn't work, we set out on a two-day trek to the group's last known whereabouts.

At noon the next day, two Meakambut men come striding into our camp. They recognize Joshua Meraveka, a member of Sullivan's team. He introduces them as John and Mark Aiyo. John is a leader of the Meakambut. While waiting there for the rest of the Embarakal to arrive, John explains cave life to me. He says they like their hunter-gatherer life and have no interest in changing it.

Before long, the rest of the Meakambut arrive. This is when we first encounter Lidia, curled up by the fire, coughing horribly. A member of our team, an emergency medical technician, examines Lidia. He determines that she likely has a life-threatening case of pneumonia and gives her double doses of antibiotics and Tylenol. We suggest that first thing in the morning she be carried out of the mountains, to a clinic in the village of Amboin. Two other Meakambut are also seriously ill.

One man from our team, Sebastian Haraha, is an ethnographer who has come to pinpoint the locations of the Meakambut's caves. He hopes to register them so the homeland of the Meakambut will be protected. Now, he volunteers to escort the sick.

Two nights later, John begins to let down his guard. He admits that his group hasn't eaten meat or killed a pig for over three months. He is deeply worried for his people. When the campfire dies out, John whispers something he wants me to pass on to the government of Papua New Guinea.

The next morning our team leaves the mountains. We reach our motor dugout and travel downstream

A member of the Meakambut tribe wearing bird-feather headdress

to the village of Awim and learn that Lidia and the others are here. Lidia is alive. Simple antibiotics have saved her.

At breakfast, I find Sebastian Haraha. "Protecting the caves? What does it matter if there are no Meakambut left?" asks Sebastian. "The Meakambut are on the edge of extinction. They are dying from easily treatable illnesses. In ten years they could be completely gone, and their culture and language would vanish. When I get back to Port Moresby, I'm going to walk straight into the prime minister's office and do something."

I nod and pass along John's message: "We, the Meakambut people, will give up hunting and always moving and living in the mountain caves if the government will give us a health clinic and a school, and two shovels and two axes, so we can build homes."

The Meakambut continue to live without access to government services. But they have partly settled in homes on the ridgetop camp of Tembakapa. Despite the threat of encroachment by miners, they continue to hunt and gather on their traditional land.

DISCUSSION

Discuss these questions with a classmate.

1. What surprised or interested you most about the culture described in the passage? Why?
2. What was the role of the anthropologists in this story? How was it similar to or different from what you learned about anthropologists and ethnologists in the lecture?
3. What information from the lecture was exemplified in the article?

RESEARCH PROJECT

Individually or in a group, research one of the following topics. Write a short paper on the topic, or plan and present a group presentation to inform the class about the topic.

1. Isolated cultures: Where do they still exist, and what challenges do they face?
2. Research in cultural anthropology: What similarities and differences exist between your culture and another?
3. Intercultural understanding: Does studying or living in another culture change an individual's values? Provide evidence to support your opinion.
4. Another related topic that interests you or your group.

UNIT 1 VIDEO The Gift of Traveling

BEFORE VIEWING

TOPIC PREVIEW

What do you think it would be like to be a professional photographer who travels around the world? Write some pros and cons of the job. Discuss your answers with a partner.

Pros	Cons

VOCABULARY PREVIEW

A **Read the definitions of these key words and phrases that you will hear during the video.**

hanging out with spending leisure time with
flexibility the ability to easily adjust to new situations
had language in common shared the same language
set up camp find a new place to start a home and live
on assignment carrying out a job you are hired to do as a journalist or photographer
compelling so interesting that you want to pay close attention to it
immerse yourself become completely involved in something
abide by follow a particular law, custom, rule, etc.
inspirational making you feel excited and have creative ideas

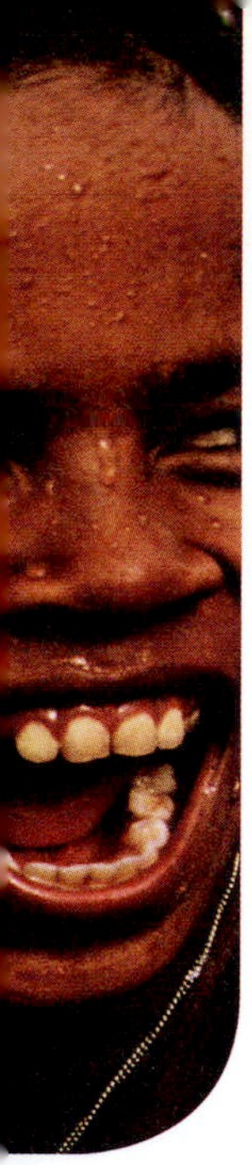

B **Work with a partner and write in the blank the word from the box that best completes the sentence.**

communities	culture	kids	photographers
spend	stories	travelers	unusual

1. Annie's children travel with her to foreign countries and ________________ a lot of time **hanging out with** ________________ from other cultures.
2. When making friends in new ________________, people don't always **have** the same **language in common**.
3. **Flexibility** is an important quality for professional ________________ **on assignment** because they might have to **set up camp** in some ________________ places.
4. Experienced ________________ know that it is important to **abide by** the customs of the culture you are visiting.
5. You can **immerse yourself** in another ________________, even if you can't speak the language.
6. When photographs are **compelling** and **inspirational**, it makes people want to read the ________________ that accompany them.

VIEWING

FIRST VIEWING

Watch the video, and then compare your first impressions with a partner. Talk about what you remember, what surprised you, and what interested you.

SECOND VIEWING

Watch the video again. Listen for the missing words and write them in the blanks.

1. Our kids have traveled to every continent except ________________. More importantly, when we travel they have lived in communities. We never stayed in ________________.
2. If you go into each culture open, and look people in the ________________ and observe and listen, you're going to make connections that are well beyond what most ________________ get to see.
3. And so the real challenge for a photographer is to bring her or his own unique ________________ to that subject ________________.
4. The camera has always given me an ________________ to walk up to people and spend time with them and even go ________________ with them.

THIRD VIEWING

Complete these notes as you watch the video. Write only important words, not full sentences, and abbreviate common words.

1. Our kids
   - trav ev cont – ______________________________
   - ______________________________
   - not always lang in comm but always fun
   - confident
   - daught 18, no probs trav
   - understand all ppl ______________________________
   - v flexible ______________________________
2. Challenge of photog
   - bring a unique ______________________________
   - tell a ______________________________
   - compel ppl to ______________________________
3. Lessons learned in trav
   - allow self to immers → ______________________________
   - ______________________________ gd lang skills
   - be a guest, i.e., follow ______________________________

AFTER VIEWING

ORAL SUMMARY

Use your notes to create an oral summary of the video with your partner. As you work together, add details to your notes that your partner included but you had missed.

DISCUSSION

Discuss the following questions with a classmate or in a small group.

1. Think about what you learned in this unit. In what ways is a photographer a type of anthropologist?
2. What is Annie Griffiths' advice for communicating with people from different cultures? Do you agree with her? Why or why not?
3. Why does Annie Griffiths say regular travel is spoiled for her?
4. After listening to Annie Griffiths, would you like to be a travel photographer? Why or why not?

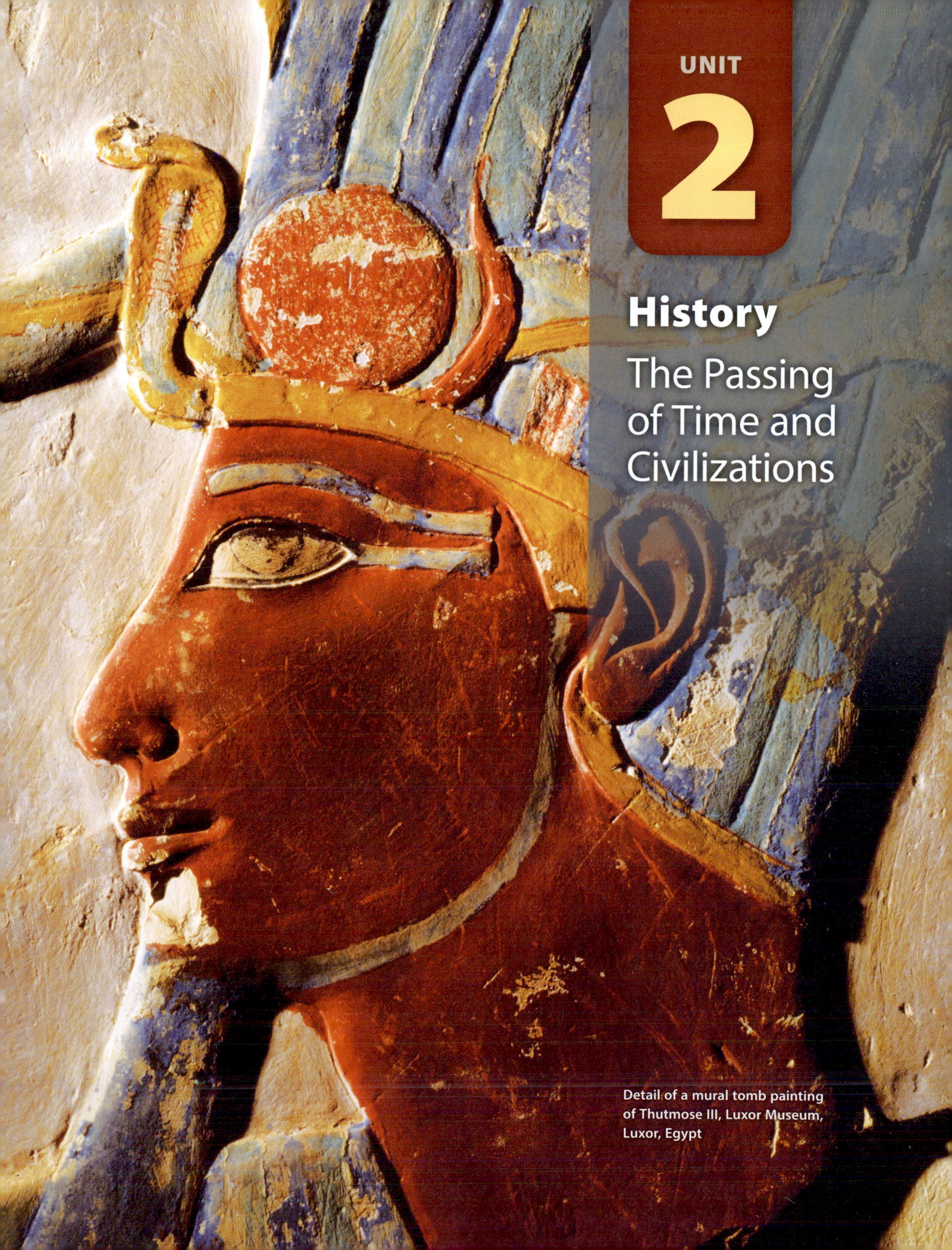

UNIT 2

History

The Passing of Time and Civilizations

Detail of a mural tomb painting of Thutmose III, Luxor Museum, Luxor, Egypt

CHAPTER

3

The Egyptian Pyramids

Houses of Eternity

TOPIC PREVIEW

Answer the following questions with a partner or your classmates.

1. What do you know about the pyramids of Egypt? Who built them? When?
2. Look at the title of this chapter. Why is a pyramid called a *house of eternity*?
3. Grave robbers are people who steal things from burial places. Why were grave robbers very interested in the pyramids?

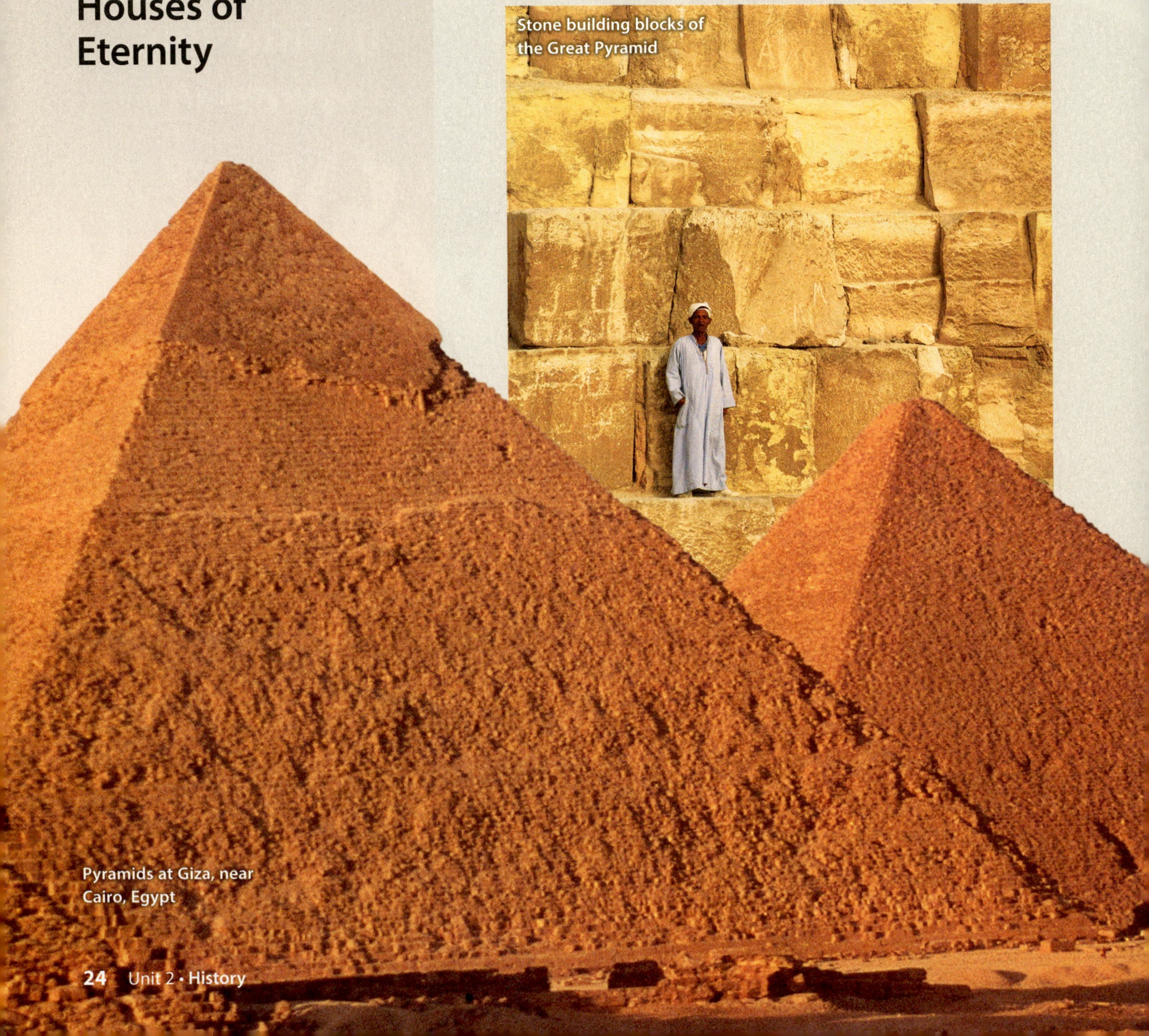
Stone building blocks of the Great Pyramid

Pyramids at Giza, near Cairo, Egypt

BEFORE LISTENING

VOCABULARY PREVIEW

CD 1, TR 13

A **Read through the sentences below, which are missing vocabulary from the lecture. Listen to the sentences and write the missing words in the blanks.**

1. To many people throughout the world, some of the most remarkable and puzzling __________________ of ancient times are the pyramids of ancient Egypt.
2. Even though many of the pyramids are in __________________, they still give us some idea of the magnificence of ancient Egypt's __________________.
3. Remember, when we're talking about ancient Egypt, we're talking about at least 30 __________________ dynasties.
4. So when a person died, and especially when a __________________ died, in order to ensure his eternal life, he had his body embalmed or __________________.
5. In other words, he had his __________________ dried out and wrapped in linen to __________________ it from decay.
6. You see, the ancient Egyptians really believed that if one's mummy was destroyed, then his or her __________________ would be destroyed.
7. For another thing, the ancient Egyptians believed that the dead person could take his or her earthly __________________ along to the next world.
8. Anyway, the dead person was provided with food, clothing, furniture, __________________, and even servants.
9. It seems that local builders and conquerors found it convenient to __________________ off the limestone from the pyramids and use it to build with.
10. And yet, what is so __________________ is that even these __________________ did not escape the attacks of the grave robbers.

B **Check the spelling of the vocabulary words with your teacher. Discuss the meanings of these words and any other unfamiliar words in the sentences.**

PREDICTIONS

Think about the questions in the Topic Preview on page 24 and the sentences you heard in the Vocabulary Preview. Write three questions that you think will be answered in the lecture. Share your questions with your classmates.

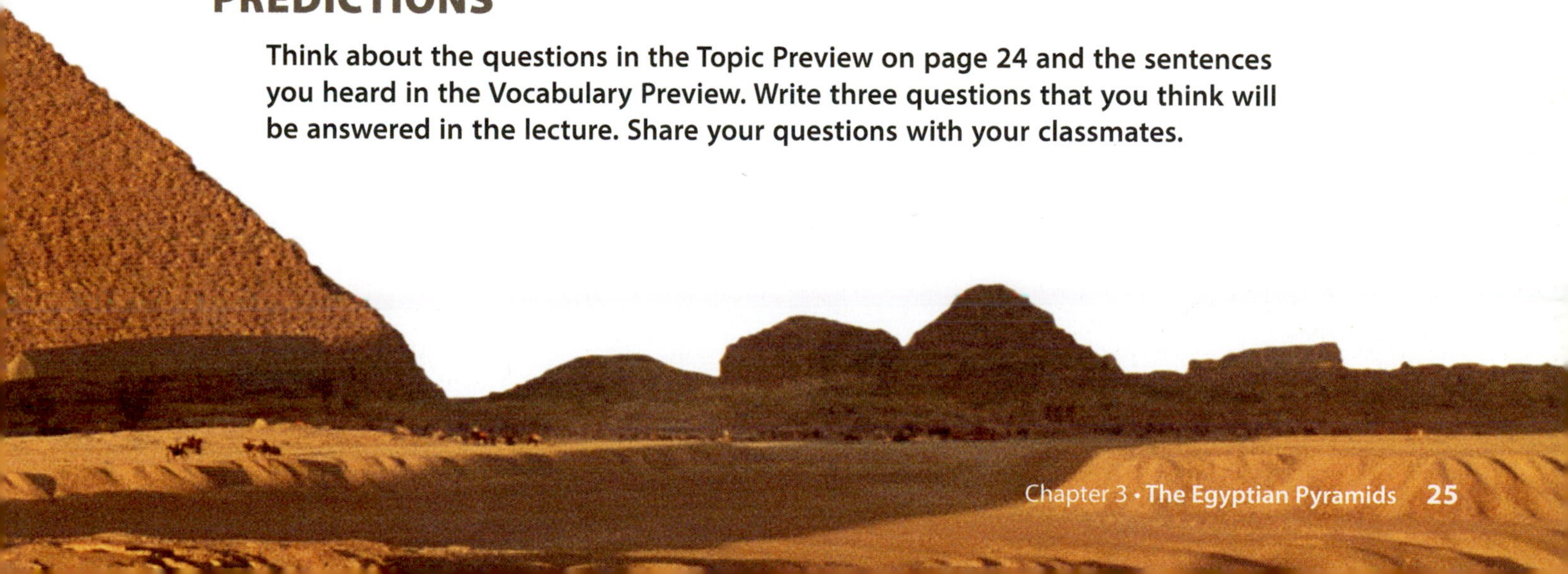

NOTETAKING PREPARATION

Recording Numbers and Dates in Notes

Lectures often include numbers and dates. There are many different ways that numbers are stated. Here are some examples:

2010	***twenty ten*** or ***two thousand and ten*** (listen for the reduced *n* instead of *and*)
2,500,000	***two and a half billion*** or ***2.5 billion*** ("2 point 5 billion")

When taking notes about numbers, the following are useful abbreviations:

2000→	since 2000	K	thousand	ht	height
←2000	until 2000	M	million	wt	weight
950–2000	from 950 to 2000	B	billion	'	foot, feet
C20	20th century	m	meter(s)	"	inch, inches
bce	before the common era	km	kilometer(s)	~	about, approximately
↓	lower, decrease, less	g	gram(s)	=	is, are, have, equals
↑	higher, increase, more	kg	kilogram(s)	≤	at least

A **Look at the notes. What do they mean?**

1. 2614–2502 bce ____________________
2. ~2.3 M ____________________
3. ~15K kg ____________________
4. ht=147m ____________________
5. 3 m ↓ ____________________
6. 2500 kg ____________________

CD 1, TR 14

B **Listen to sentences from the lecture. Take notes. Use symbols and abbreviations where possible.**

1. ____________________
2. ____________________
3. ____________________
4. ____________________
5. ____________________
6. ____________________

FIRST LISTENING

CD 1, TR 15

Listen to the lecture and number the slides on this page and the next in the order they would be shown during the lecture. Write the number of the slide on the line provided and answer the question to the right of the slide.

Lesser Pyramids

Later Dynasties
1786 BCE

Slide #_____

What is the area called where these tombs were found?

Evolution of Pyramids

Third Dynasty
2664–2615 BCE

Slide #_____

What is the name of this type of pyramid?

Great Pyramids

Fourth Dynasty
2614–2502 BCE

Slide #____

Where are these pyramids?

Structure of Pyramids

First and Second Dynasties
3100–2665 BCE

Slide #____

What is the name of the type of tomb the pharaohs first built?

The Pyramids of Egypt

What do the ruins of the pyramids show us about ancient Egyptian civilization?

- Belief in the afterlife
- Grave robbers common

Slide #____

Why were the pyramids built?

SECOND LISTENING

CD 1, TR 16

Now that you've listened to the lecture once, listen to it again and take notes. Write on a separate piece of paper.

THIRD LISTENING

CD 1, TR 17

You will hear parts of the lecture again. Look through your notes as you listen. A notetaking mentor will discuss the notes. Circle the answer that is closest to the notes you took, and put a check (✓) next to the notes that the mentor wrote.

Part 1

1. a. *Egypt* b. *Eg.* c. *E.* d. *Egy*
2. a. *the pyramids* b. *pyds* c. *P's* d. *pyr's*
3. a. *3,000 yrs.* b. *300 years* c. *3K yrs* d. *three thousand years*
4. a. *dyn. = series K's & Q's* b. *dyn.: Romanovs, Ming, Al-Saud*

Part 2

5. a. *bench* b. *shoebox* c. *low, flat* d. *rect.*

Part 3

6. a.

"typical" pyr
- 3rd Dyn – 2664–2614
- King ~~So~~ Zoser
- arch. = Imhotep
- "step" pyr = pile mastabas

b.

Next style – typical
- 3rd dyn
- Zoser, Imhotep

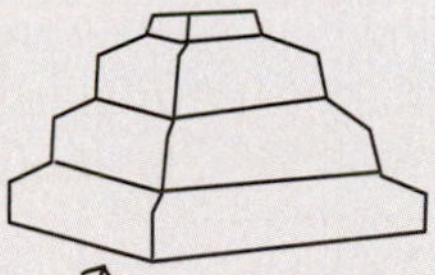

c.

B. the "typical" pyramid was built in Third Dynasty (2664–2615 BCE)
1. Built for King ZOSER by architect [IMH]???
2. pile of mastabas

AFTER LISTENING

ACCURACY CHECK

CD 1, TR 18

You will hear questions about the lecture. Answer each question by referring to the notes that you took while listening to the lecture.

1. a. 20
   b. 30
   c. 40
2. a. to remember the pharaohs
   b. to send the pharoahs into the afterlife
   c. to show people the wealth of the pharaohs
3. a. servants
   b. clothing
   c. a pyramid
4. a. underground
   b. mastaba
   c. step
5. a. near Cairo
   b. in Alexandria
   c. Luxor
6. a. Khufu
   b. Cheops
   c. King
7. a. 2.3 million
   b. 2,500
   c. 15,000
8. a. It was a step pyramid.
   b. It was underground.
   c. It was in Giza.

ORAL SUMMARY

Use your notes to create an oral summary of the lecture with a partner. As you work together, add details to your notes that your partner had included but which you had missed.

DISCUSSION

Discuss the following questions with a classmate or in a small group.

1. The construction of pyramids was an example of the search for everlasting life. In what other ways have people searched for immortality?
2. Why did King Thutmose I decide not to be buried in a pyramid? In what other ways do you think the Egyptian pharaohs could have solved the problems they encountered with their system of burial?
3. What do you think is the most interesting structure in the world? The Eiffel Tower? The Great Wall of China? A structure in your country? List three reasons why you find this structure interesting and share these reasons with a partner.

EXPANSION

PRE-READING

The following Reading is about the Egyptian pharaoh Ramses II. Before you read, answer the following questions. Share your answers with a classmate.

1. Using the information about pharaohs from the lecture, write three statements you expect to be true about Ramses II.
2. In the lecture, the speaker mentioned that the pharaohs were mummified. What do you remember about this technique for preserving bodies? If you could learn three more things about mummification, what would you want to find out?

READING

Now read the article.

Ramses the Great

On my last day in Egypt I finally receive permission from the Egyptian Antiquities Organization to see Ramses' mummy. My colleague, Lou Mazzatenta, is also permitted to photograph the pharaoh. At the Egyptian Museum in Cairo, conservation director Nasry Iskander lifts the dark velvet off the mummy case. I behold the face. Browned and chisel sharp. Arms crossed regally across the chest. A long neck, a proud aquiline nose, and wisps of reddish hair, probably colored by his embalmers.

Ramses' mummification and burial rites likely took the traditional 70 days. Embalmers removed internal organs, placing the liver, lungs, stomach, and intestines in sacred jars. His heart was sealed in his body. Egyptians believed that it was the source of intellect as well as feeling and would be required for the final judgment. Only if a heart was as light as the feather of truth would the god Osiris receive its owner into the afterlife.

Egyptians did not appreciate the brain. The embalmers drew it out through the nose and threw it away.

After they dried the corpse with natron salt, the embalmers washed the body and coated it with preserving resins. Finally they wrapped it in hundreds of yards of linen.

Mummy of Ramses II in the Egyptian Museum, Cairo

Within 150 years of Ramses' burial, his tomb was robbed by thieves and his mummy desecrated. Twice reburied by priests, the body retained some of its secrets. X-ray examination of the body indicated that Ramses suffered badly from arthritis in the hip, which would have forced him to stoop. His teeth were severely worn, and he had dental abscesses and gum disease.

The photography finished, the velvet is replaced over Ramses' mummy—but the face stays with me. Not the face of Shelley's Ozymandias, not that of a god, but the face of a man. Was Ramses bombastic, cruel, ego driven? By our standards, certainly. He left no evidence of the human complexity or the bitterly learned insights that redeem such proudful mythic kings as Oedipus, or Shakespeare's King Lear, but he did love deeply and lose. And all those children who died before him—Ramses knew human suffering. Did he really believe he was a god? Who can say? But clearly, he strove to be the king his country expected—providing wealth and security—and succeeded. More than most, this man got what he wanted.

Sarcophagus containing the mummy of Pharaoh Ramses II

DISCUSSION

Discuss these questions with a classmate.

1. What surprised or interested you most about the mummification process described in the passage? Why?
2. How was the information in the reading similar to or different from the information in the lecture?
3. Summarize what you have learned about beliefs of ancient Egyptians from both the lecture and the article.

RESEARCH PROJECT

Individually or in a group, research one of the following topics. Write a short paper on the topic or plan and present a group presentation to inform the class about the topic.

1. The discovery of the tomb of the boy pharaoh, King Tutankhamen
2. The pyramid of Cheops
3. The pyramids of Mayan and Aztec culture in South America
4. The life of Ramses II or another ancient Egyptian king or queen
5. Another question that interests you or your group

CHAPTER

4

The First Emperor of China

Building an Empire and a House of Eternity

TOPIC PREVIEW

Answer the following questions with a partner or your classmates.

1. Look at the title of this chapter. The first emperor of China was named Qin Shi Huang. How does a leader of a country build an empire?
2. Look at the photo. Why do you think the emperor had statues of soldiers in his tomb?
3. What are some differences you can see between this "House of Eternity" and the Pyramids?

Terra-cotta warriors from the tomb complex of Qin Shi Huang

BEFORE LISTENING

VOCABULARY PREVIEW

CD 2, TR 1

A **Read through the sentences below, which are missing vocabulary from the lecture. Listen to the sentences and write the missing words in the blanks.**

1. ________________ find out about these ancient times by studying the ruins of cities, monuments, or tombs, or any written records that remain.
2. The history part of my talk will be about Qin Shi Huang, who was the ________________ of the first unified empire in China.
3. Today, I'm also going to be talking about what has been found, to ________________, in the area of Qin Shi Huang's tomb.
4. Before Qin Shi Huang unified the empire in 221 BCE, China had been torn apart by wars between seven regional ________________.
5. When Qin Shi Huang became Emperor, he decreed that a ________________ system of Chinese ________________ was to be used throughout the empire.
6. In the second year after unification, ________________ of three major ________________ highways was begun.
7. At this point, I'm going to ________________ from talking about the ________________ of Qin Shi Huang to the archaeology part of my lecture.
8. It seems that as soon as the Emperor gained power, he became ________________ with death, and with constructing a magnificent House of Eternity for his afterlife.
9. The entire area of the tomb covers ________________ 56.25 square kilometers.
10. It is even believed that ________________ was pumped through the tomb to create the image of flowing rivers in the tomb area.
11. Without a doubt, the most striking ________________ of the Emperor Qin's House of Eternity are the ________________ warriors and horses found in the tomb area.
12. Chinese officials say that the tomb mound of the first Chinese emperor will not be ________________ until preservation techniques have advanced significantly.

B **Check the spelling of the vocabulary words with your teacher. Discuss the meanings of these words and any other unfamiliar words in the sentences.**

PREDICTIONS

Think about the questions in the Topic Preview on page 33 and the sentences you heard in the Vocabulary Preview. Write three questions that you think will be answered in the lecture. Share your questions with your classmates.

NOTETAKING PREPARATION

Using Indentation and Spacing Effectively in Notes

When you take notes, your use of space on the page can help you review your notes. Here are some tips:

- Align information that has the same level of importance. For example, begin main ideas on the left margin of your paper. Indent supporting information.
- Leave extra space on one side to add more information or notes later.
- Skip one line between ideas. Skip several lines to show a new topic.
- Don't worry about trying to make a formal outline of a lecture. Very few lecturers follow an outline.

A **Look at the notes below and answer the questions.**

1. Identify the main idea.
2. Identify two specific points.
3. Why is there space in the middle of the last line and question marks at the end? Where do you think the notetaker can find out the missing information?

Q.S, unif. emp. 221 bce – def. 6 K'doms
  1. end pwr 6 K'doms
  2. centr. imp. syst., → > [   ] yrs   ???

CD 2, TR 2

B **Listen to the part of the lecture for the notes in A above. Fill in the missing information. Then rewrite the notes below in the space provided so the notes show main ideas and specific facts more effectively.**

QS unif. & prot. emp. 1st, stand'ize
syst char. 2nd 1 syst. wts. & meas., 1 syst. curr.

FIRST LISTENING

CD 2, TR 3

Listen to the lecture and number the slides on this page and the next in the order they would be shown during the lecture. Write the number of the slide on the line provided and answer the question to the right of the slide.

Unification

Standardization of systems in the empire

Protection of the empire

- Ordered building of Great Wall

Slide #____

What was the first thing that Qin Shi Huang standardized?

Construction of Tomb

Replica of Qin capital

Terra-cotta warriors and horses

Slide #____

What was used to resemble a flowing river?

First Emperor of China
Building an Empire and a House of Eternity

History ↔ Archaeology

Qin Shi Huang ↔ Tomb

Slide #_____

When was Qin Shi Huang's tomb discovered?

Excavation of Tomb

Museum (1975) covers 3 pits of excavation site

Slide #_____

Have archaeologists finished excavating the entire tomb?

Historical Context

China – divided into regional kingdoms
- Ying Zheng – King of Qin

Qin unified China
- Centralized imperial system begins
- Lasts 2,000 years

Slide #_____

How many kingdoms did Ying Zheng defeat?

SECOND LISTENING

CD 2, TR 4

Now that you've listened to the lecture once, listen to it again and take notes. Write on a separate piece of paper.

THIRD LISTENING

CD 2, TR 5

You will hear parts of the lecture again. Look through your notes as you listen. A notetaking mentor will discuss the notes. Circle the answer below which is closest to the notes you took, and put a check (✓) next to the notes that the mentor wrote.

Part 1

1. a.

to protect empire – Great Wall of China
already 3 walls – joined 1500 miles
also 3 highways – 6,800 km (4,225 miles)

b.

to protect E. –
GWall
• 3 sm. walls bef.
• 1500 mi.
3 hwys
• 6800 km

Part 2

2. a.

3 maj. hwys
• 6800 km
> Rom. E. rds

b.

3 hwys
• 6800 km / 4225 mi
150 C.E. Rom E. rds
• 5,984 km / 3718 mi

3. a.

> Rom. E. rds
+ constr. proj. = tomb
bio. → arch

b.

> Rom. E. rds
tomb/maus.
preoc. w/ death
arch.

c.

> Rom. E. rds
tomb

Part 2 – (arch.) QS's tomb

AFTER LISTENING

ACCURACY CHECK

CD 2, TR 6

You will hear questions about the lecture. Answer each question by referring to the notes that you took while listening to the lecture.

1. a. 210 BCE
   b. 215 BCE
   c. 259 BCE
2. a. 215 BCE
   b. 259 BCE
   c. 221 BCE
3. a. to standardize things
   b. to unify the empire
   c. to protect his empire
4. a. 500 miles
   b. 1,500 miles
   c. 5,000 miles
5. a. 6,800
   b. 68,000
   c. 700,000
6. a. 11 years
   b. 17 years
   c. 70 years
7. a. 56.25 square kilometers
   b. 12,000 square meters
   c. 16,300 square meters
8. a. dead soldiers
   b. ancient rivers
   c. mercury

ORAL SUMMARY

Use your notes to create an oral summary of the lecture with a partner. As you work together, add details to your notes that your partner had included but which you had missed.

DISCUSSION

Discuss the following questions with a classmate or in a small group.

1. Provide examples of the changes Qin Shi Huang made when he became emperor. Why were these changes necessary and important?
2. The lecturer says it is necessary to set the historical context for understanding the archaeological find of Qin Shi Huang's terra-cotta army. Why is knowing the historical context important for modern-day archaeologists and tourists to the site?
3. Explain what is holding up full excavation of the Emperor's tomb. When do archaeologists suspect the tomb may be fully excavated? In the near or distant future? Why?
4. Discuss the ways in which the pharaohs of ancient Egypt and the emperors of ancient China were similar and different in terms of their views of life and death and their preparation for the afterlife.

PRE-READING

The following Reading is about the discovery and excavation of the tomb of Qin Shi Huang. Before you read, answer the following questions. Share your answers with a classmate.

1. Look at the title and headings in the article. Write two ways in which this article will be similar to the lecture and two ways in which it may be different.
2. In the lecture, the speaker only gave the dates when the tomb was discovered. If you could learn two more things about this, what would you want to find out?

READING

Now read the article.

Terra-Cotta Army Protects First Emperor's Tomb

Workers digging a well outside the city of Xi'an, China, in 1974 struck upon one of the greatest archaeological discoveries in the world: a life-size clay soldier poised for battle. The diggers notified Chinese authorities, who dispatched government archaeologists to the site. They found not one, but thousands of clay soldiers, each with unique facial expressions and positioned according to rank. And though largely gray today, patches of paint hint at once brightly colored clothes. Further excavations have revealed swords, arrow tips, and other weapons, many in pristine condition.

The soldiers are in trenchlike, underground corridors. In some of the corridors, clay horses are aligned four abreast; behind them are wooden chariots. The terra-cotta army, as it is known, is part of an elaborate mausoleum created to accompany the first emperor of China into the afterlife, according to archaeologists.

Young Emperor

Ying Zheng took the throne in 246 BC at the age of 13. By 221 BC he had unified a collection of warring kingdoms and taken the name of Qin Shi Huang Di—the First Emperor of Qin. During his rule, Qin standardized coins, weights, and measures; interlinked the states with canals and roads; and is credited for building the first version of the Great Wall.

According to writings of court historian Siam Qian during the following Han dynasty, Qin ordered the mausoleum's construction shortly after taking the throne. More than 700,000 laborers worked on the project, which was halted in 209 BC amid uprisings a year after Qin's death.

To date, four pits have been partially excavated. Three are filled with the terra-cotta soldiers, horse-drawn chariots, and weapons. The fourth pit is empty, a testament to the original unfinished construction. Archaeologists estimate the pits may contain as many as 8,000 figures, but the total may never be known.

Unexcavated Tomb

Qin's tomb itself remains unexcavated, though Siam Qian's writings suggest even greater treasures. "The tomb was filled with models of palaces, pavilions and offices as well as fine vessels, precious stones and rarities," reads a translation of the text. The account indicates the tomb contains replicas of the area's rivers and streams made with mercury flowing to the sea through hills and mountains of bronze. Precious stones such as pearls are said to represent the sun, moon, and other stars.

Modern tests on the tomb mound have revealed unusually high concentrations of mercury, lending credence to at least some of the historical account. Chinese archaeologists are also using remote-sensing technology to probe the tomb mound. The technique recently revealed an underground chamber with four stairlike walls. An archaeologist working on the site told the Chinese press that the chamber may have been built for the soul of the emperor.

Pieces of the terra-cotta army are still being recovered and assembled.

Experimental pits dug around the tomb have revealed dancers, musicians, and acrobats full of life and caught in mid-performance, a sharp contrast to the military poses of the famous terra-cotta soldiers. But further excavations of the tomb itself are on hold, at least for now. "It is best to keep the ancient tomb untouched, because of the complex conditions inside," Duan Qinbao, a researcher with the Shaanxi Provincial Archaeology Institute, told the *China Daily* in 2006.

DISCUSSION

Discuss these questions with a classmate.

1. What surprised or interested you most about the discovery and excavation work described in the passage? Why?
2. How was the information in the article similar to or different from the information in the lecture?
3. Summarize what you have learned about the first emperor of China and his House of Eternity from both the lecture and the article.

RESEARCH PROJECT

Individually or in a group, research one of the following topics. Write a short paper on the topic or plan and present a group presentation to inform the class about the topic.

1. Future excavation of the Emperor's tomb. What is holding it up? Will it ever be fully excavated?
2. The archaeological process of unearthing the tombs and artifacts
3. Another great archaeological discovery
4. Another related topic that interests you or your group

UNIT 2

VIDEO Palenque

BEFORE VIEWING

TOPIC PREVIEW

Name an ancient site that you have visited or that you know about. Write three facts about this site. Then share your information with a partner.

Site: ______________________________

____

____

____

VOCABULARY PREVIEW

A Read the definitions of these key words that you will hear during the video.

inscriptions writing carved into metal or stone
mason a skilled person who makes or builds things with stone or bricks
slab a thick, flat piece of something such as a large, smooth area of stone
altar a table or other raised, flat surface, used for religious ceremonies
hollow having empty space on the inside; not solid
jacks tools for lifting heavy items such as cars
reconstructed put something together again that was broken apart
aura a feeling that comes from a person, place, or thing

B **Work with a partner and write vocabulary from A in the blanks in the sentences.**

1. We know from the ________________ that Pakal, one the greatest of all Maya kings, was born in the year 603 AD.
2. A stone structure with a flat top looked like an ________________, but the archaeologists weren't sure what it was.
3. The head ________________ suggested drilling a hole in the side of the stone structure to see if it was ________________.
4. The archaeologists used 15 automobile ________________ to lift up the heavy stone ________________.
5. The ancient palace has an incredible ________________ about it; everyone who visits is amazed.

VIEWING

FIRST VIEWING

Watch the video, and then compare your first impressions with a partner. Talk about what you remember, what surprised you, and what interested you.

SECOND VIEWING

Watch the video again. Listen for the missing words and write them in the blanks.

1. As you can see from this wonderful photograph, the site itself—Palenque—sits on a kind of a ________________.
2. The floor of the temple was made out of big, stone slabs with ________________ in them. So Alberto had the workers pull up the ________________.
3. We went into town and got 15 automobile jacks and pulled the thing up, and there was a ________________ inside.
4. His full name was K'inich Janaab' Pakal, and he was the ________________ king of Palenque, one of the greatest of all Maya kings.
5. He was covered in jade, as a good Maya king would be. A jade collar, jade bracelets, and an ________________ mask as well.
6. Years and years after he's dead, Pakal is still at the ________________ of everything.

Jade death mask of King Pakal

THIRD VIEWING

Complete the time lines as you watch the video. Write your notes next to the dates.

Palenque archeology

1934

1948 – started

– summer

1952 – June

Pakal

603 AD

615 AD

Today

AFTER VIEWING

ORAL SUMMARY

Use your notes to create an oral summary of the video with a partner. As you work together, add details to your notes that your partner included but you had missed.

DISCUSSION

Discuss the following questions with a classmate or in a small group.

1. What do you know about other ancient burial practices? In what ways was the burial of the Mayan King Pakal similar or different?
2. Who was Juan Chablé? Why was he important to this project?
3. Why does David Stuart say that Palenque is "Pakal City"?
4. After listening to this lecture, do you think you would like to be an archaeologist? Why or why not?

UNIT 3

Sociology

The Changing World of Work

Office block at night in Dusseldorf, Germany

CHAPTER

5

The Distributed Workforce

Where and When People Work

TOPIC PREVIEW

Answer the following questions with a partner or your classmates.

1. In what ways do you think the world of work is changing?
2. If you could choose to work either at an office or at home, which would you pick? Why? What are some of the advantages and disadvantages of working from home rather than at an office?
3. Look at the title of this chapter. What does *distributed* mean? What is a *workforce*? What do you think "the distributed workforce" is?

Two young men conduct business hanging from trees!

BEFORE LISTENING

VOCABULARY PREVIEW

CD 2, TR 7

A **Read through the sentences below, which are missing vocabulary from the lecture. Listen to the sentences and write the missing words in the blanks.**

1. Employees may be based in a traditional office; or they might work from home—so-called ________________; or they could be ________________ employees, such as salespeople.
2. Employees working outside of the office need access from remote locations to company ________________ and to stay connected with the use of ________________ technology.
3. Full-time employees often expect ________________ such as health insurance, and they might be difficult to ________________.

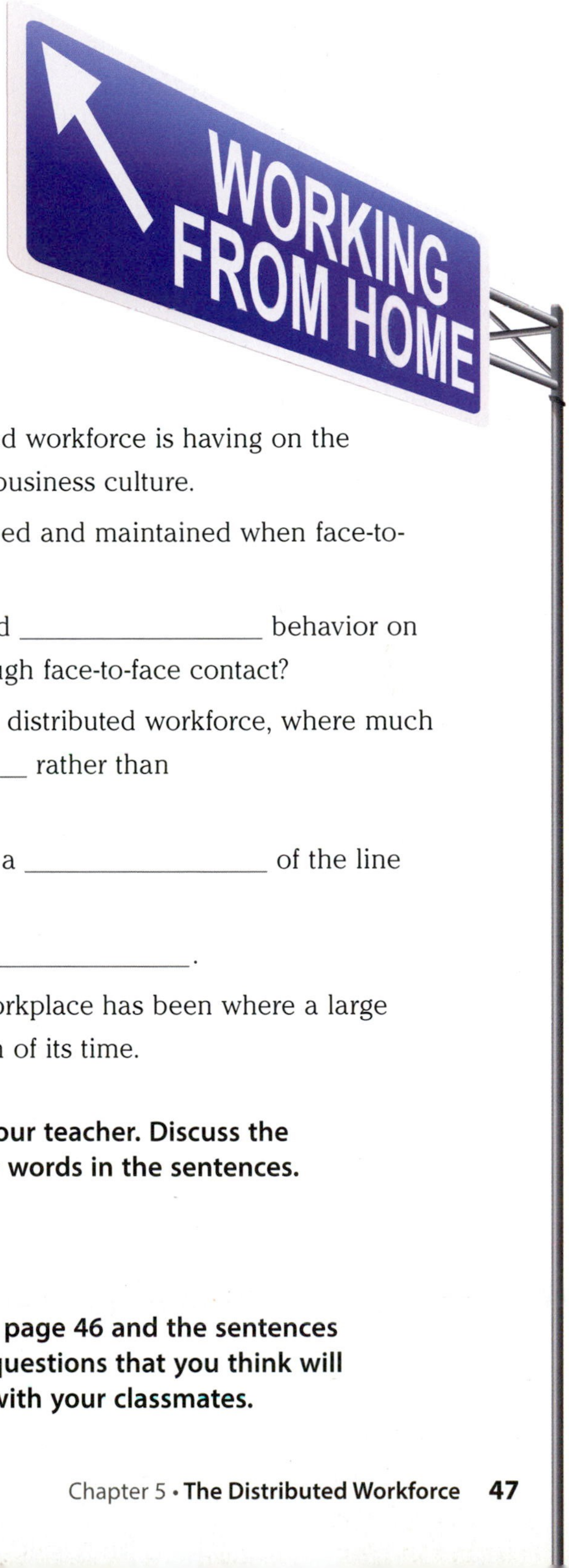

4. It is not yet understood what impact a distributed workforce is having on the ________________ yet vital development of a business culture.
5. How can group ________________ be developed and maintained when face-to-face meetings are rare or ________________?
6. How dependent are qualities such as loyalty and ________________ behavior on personal relationships that are established through face-to-face contact?
7. Can personal relationships truly evolve across a distributed workforce, where much of the work is conducted in a ________________ rather than physical environment?
8. When workers are available 24–7, it can lead to a ________________ of the line between work and personal life.
9. In a ________________ world, there is no ________________.
10. Since the Industrial ________________, the workplace has been where a large proportion of the adult population spends much of its time.

B **Check the spelling of the vocabulary words with your teacher. Discuss the meanings of these words and any other unfamiliar words in the sentences.**

PREDICTIONS

Think about the questions in the Topic Preview on page 46 and the sentences you heard in the Vocabulary Preview. Write three questions that you think will be answered in the lecture. Share your questions with your classmates.

NOTETAKING PREPARATION

Using Intonation to Identify New Main Points

A lecturer who has completed a main point and is ready to move on to a new point will often use very marked falling intonation, followed by a long pause.

The technology is here and it's here to **stay**. [long pause]

Signal words and phrases such as *next*, *another*, and *on the other hand* also indicate that the lecturer is moving from one main point to another. Often these signal words have strong rising intonation.

. . . and it's here to stay. [long pause] **On the oth**er hand . . .

The combination of marked falling intonation, a long pause, and a rising signal word should alert you to the fact that a new main point is about to be introduced.

CD 2, TR 8

A **Listen to the intonation in these sentences from the lecture. Has the lecturer finished talking about one main point and is now about to introduce a new one? Circle *a* or *b*.**

The lecturer will

1. a. introduce a new point b. continue with same point
2. a. introduce a new point b. continue with same point
3. a. introduce a new point b. continue with same point

CD 2, TR 9

B **Listen to the sentences. This time you will hear how the lecturer continues and if a new main point is introduced. As you listen, check and see if you chose the correct answers in A above.**

LISTENING

FIRST LISTENING

CD 2, TR 10

Listen to the lecture and number the slides on this page and the next in the order they would be shown during the lecture. Write the number of the slide on the line provided and answer the question to the right of the slide.

The Distributed Workforce

Geography

Working arrangements

Technology

Slide #____

What is a *distributed workforce*?

Advantages

Employers

- Local workforce
- Flexibility

Employees

- Location
- Schedule

Slide #____

A distributed workforce has what obvious advantage to a global business?

Impact on Society

Humans as social beings

Face-to-face interaction

Work/Private life

Slide #_____

What do some distance workers feel about the loss of informal social networks?

Disadvantages

Employers

- Impact on business culture

Employees

- 24–7 availability
- Lack of job security

Slide #_____

What problem can the blurring of the line between work and personal life lead to?

Importance of Technology

Remote access

Communications technology

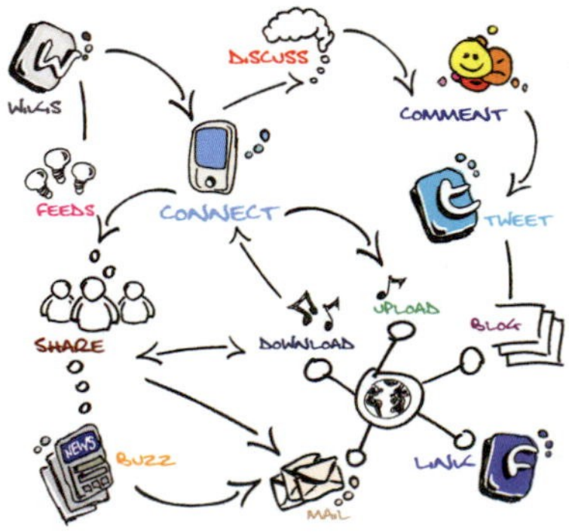

Slide #_____

How important is technology to a business with a distributed workforce?

SECOND LISTENING

CD 2, TR 11

Now that you've listened to the lecture once, listen to it again and take notes. Write on a separate piece of paper.

THIRD LISTENING

CD 2, TR 12

You will hear parts of the lecture again. Look through your notes as you listen. A notetaking mentor will discuss the notes. Circle the answer that is closest to the notes you took, and put a check (✓) next to the notes that the mentor wrote.

Part 1

1. a.

Wrkers ++
1. tech → wrk fr anywhere
2. indep contrct – + contrl wrk lives

b.

Benefits to wrkers
1. Tech make poss wrk to wrker, not wrker to job
2. stay close to fam & friends
3. indep contrac – + contrl wrk lives

Part 2

2. a.

Distance wrkrs

b.

Office wrkers

c.

Infrml support NWs

3. a.

Distance wrkrs
1. no offce → loss of soc NW ↓ isolation & ↓ support
2. + freedm BUT blur prvt/work

b.

Distance wrkrs
1. no offce → loss of soc NW
2. isolation & ↓ support
3. + freedm
4. xtra hrs eve & wkends

c.

Distance wrkrs
1. no offce → loss of soc NW ↓ isolation & ↓ support
2. blur bet. prvt/work
3. xtra hrs. eve & wkends

Part 3

4. a.

Flex Cost – Disadv
1. job sec (temp wrkrs/consul) – no ben (EX health ins)
2. Telecomm ↑ work, ↓ pay than offc wrkrs

b.

Disadv – Wrkrs
1. –job sec (temp wrkrs/consul)
2. no ben (EX health ins)
3. Telecomm ↑ work, ↓ pay than offc wrkrs

AFTER LISTENING

ACCURACY CHECK

CD 2, TR 13

You will hear questions about the lecture. Answer each question by referring to the notes that you took while listening to the lecture.

1. a. a business person
   b. a globally connected worker
   c. an office worker
2. a. a 24–7, globally connected world
   b. technological change and globalization
   c. a trend in the evolution of work
3. a. Most workers are telecommuters.
   b. Most employees don't have offices.
   c. Working arrangements vary.
4. a. workers' knowledge of local culture
   b. decreased cost of employing workers
   c. lower travel costs
5. a. flexibility
   b. better pay
   c. not having to relocate
6. a. less job security
   b. being able to terminate workers
   c. the impact on group cohesion
7. a. lack of flexibility
   b. fewer jobs being available
   c. work-related stress
8. a. better working conditions
   b. social isolation of workers
   c. decreased worker productivity

ORAL SUMMARY

Use your notes to create an oral summary of the lecture with your partner. As you work together, add details to your notes that your partner included but you had missed.

DISCUSSION

Discuss the following questions with a classmate or in a small group.

1. What are some potential advantages or disadvantages of a distributed workforce that were not mentioned in the lecture?
2. Do you think that the growth of a distributed workforce is likely to be better for employers or for employees? Why?
3. The lecturer raises a question about how group cohesion can be developed and maintained when many workers never meet face-to-face. What do you think? How can this be done?
4. Of the various employment arrangements discussed in the lecture—consulting, mobile work, telecommuting, temporary work, traditional office-based work—which do you prefer? Why?

EXPANSION

PRE-READING

The following Reading is about the impact that virtual reality games are having on the business world. Before you read, answer the following questions. Share your answers with a classmate.

1. What are virtual reality games? Do you play any virtual reality games such as *Second Life*?
2. How do you think businesses can use virtual reality games to develop and promote real-world products and services?

READING

Now read the article.

"Second Life," Other Virtual Worlds Reshaping Human Interaction

Every day millions of personal computer (PC) gamers plug into online worlds. In the game *Second Life*, online entrepreneurs can buy and sell digital real estate, create their own lines of clothing and clothing accessories, and hold virtual concerts, lectures, and sporting events. Now, as the game has grown in popularity, many corporations are eager to follow the lead of independent retailers in becoming part of the phenomenon.

Observers say that someday virtual worlds such as *Second Life* could reshape global commerce and perhaps even the way people interact over the Internet. "Imagine a future where virtual reality and the real world blend together," said Edward Castronova, associate professor of telecommunications at Indiana University in Bloomington. "It is a real possibility, and it just takes an ordinary PC."

The popularity of MMORPGs (massively multiplayer online role-playing games), which mix real and unreal worlds, is one of the main factors shaping this digital revolution. One of the most popular games, *World of Warcraft*, "is played by about 7 million members worldwide, and on any given day there are at least a few million players online," Castronova said.

Second Life, created by San Francisco, California-based Linden Lab, uses the same concept as MMORPGs. It offers a virtual environment where people—as avatars—can interact in real time. But unlike *Warcraft*, which focuses mostly on fighting monsters and completing quests, *Second Life* is built and owned entirely by its nearly 900,000 residents.

According to Castronova, the real impact of virtual worlds is the daily creation and trade of electronic assets. For instance, a *Second Life* user can build a functional piano out of virtual building blocks with various physical and behavioral properties. Some members have created their own designer flying vehicles, while others have opened up skydiving operations or built entire airports.

A *Second Life* player points to her avatar.

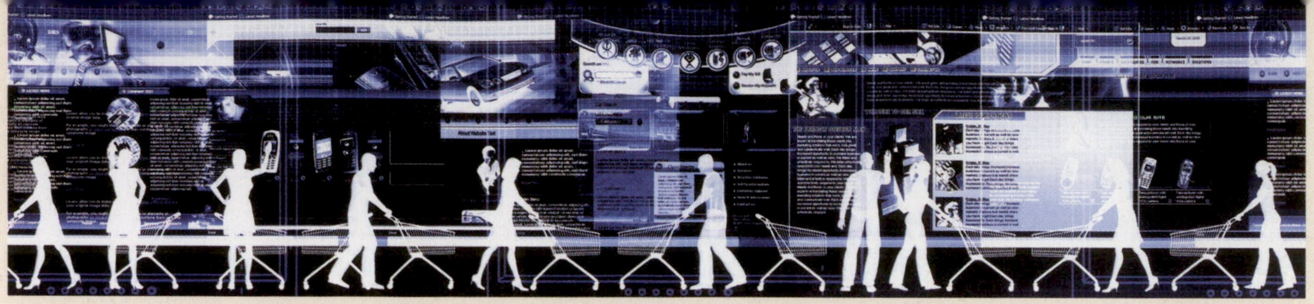

Second Life assigns intellectual property rights for all objects to their creators, meaning that the virtual objects can be sold or traded within the environment. Avatars earn an in-game currency called Linden Dollars—money that has an exchange rate and can be traded for hard cash in the real world. According to one estimate, players spend an average of $350,000 (U.S.) a day, or $130 million a year, according to Reuters.

Jerry Paffendorf is a futurist for the virtually based firm, Electric Sheep Company. Paffendorf and 25 others in the company all earn their living off virtual worlds, mostly *Second Life*. "It's a full-time job," he said. "We're the largest such team in *Second Life*." The company also facilitates trade through a Web site called SLBoutique, an Amazon.com–like marketplace for user-created content in *Second Life*. A few products and services have already established brand recognition in the game, and it is entirely possible for such virtual brands to someday actually be sold in real-world operations, Paffendorf says. "Firms could prototype and test products inside a virtual environment," he explained.

It's an intriguing thought that virtual products that have been conceived, patented, tested, bought, and sold in an online game environment might one day become real products sold in the real world.

DISCUSSION

Discuss these questions with a classmate.

1. The article talks about how virtual worlds are "reshaping human interaction." What are some of the ways that human interaction is being reshaped in the workplace as discussed in the article and the lecture?
2. Given what you learned in the lecture, what are some potential advantages to employers of using virtual environments such as *Second Life* for business purposes? The disadvantages?
3. What are some of the potential advantages to employees of using a virtual environment for business purposes? The disadvantages?

RESEARCH PROJECT

Individually or in a group, research one of the following topics. Write a short paper on the topic or plan and present a group presentation to inform the class about the topic.

1. Workforce trends in your country or another country in which you are interested
2. Companies that are using *Second Life* for business purposes
3. Innovative workplace designs, for example, open-plan office space and the use of the "third space," such as coffee shops and airport terminals, as work spaces
4. The ways some workers are trying to reduce their environmental impact through their job choices

CHAPTER

6

Age and Work

The Graying of the Workforce

TOPIC PREVIEW

Answer the following questions with a partner or your classmates.

1. Look at the title of this chapter and the photograph. What trend do you think "the graying of the workforce" refers to?
2. At what age do people typically retire in your culture? Is it common for people who are older than 65 to continue working? Is there a mandatory retirement age?
3. Who is the oldest person you know who is still working?

Old man working in his paddy field located at Alor Setar, Kedah, Malaysia

VOCABULARY PREVIEW

CD 3, TR 1

A Read through the sentences below, which are missing vocabulary from the lecture. Listen to the sentences and write the missing words in the blanks.

1. The human ________________ is also increasing: the National Institute on Aging reports that most countries show a steady increase in ________________.
2. A falling ________________ in countries with advanced economies has contributed to a rapid increase in the age of the world's population.
3. The reasons for the ________________ birthrate require a bit of explanation.
4. The need for cheap labor to work the land, coupled with high infant ________________, made large families advantageous.
5. During industrialization, there was a population ________________ from rural to urban areas.
6. Advances in ________________ technology allowed couples to take a more active role in planning their families.
7. In many developed nations, the birthrate has now fallen to below ________________ levels.
8. The ________________ rate in many European countries is now less than 1.5 children per woman.
9. The elderly support ________________ is calculated by dividing the number of working-age people by the number of people 65 or older.
10. A second impact is caused by just the opposite ________________, the large number of baby boomers who are and will be retiring at the same time, taking with them knowledge and ________________ that will be difficult to replace over the short term.
11. ________________ can occur when workers with such widely different life experiences and attitudes toward work interact.
12. Some companies have had to ________________ back expansion due to a lack of workers.

B Check the spelling of the vocabulary words with your teacher. Discuss the meanings of these words and any other unfamiliar words in the sentences.

PREDICTIONS

Think about the questions in the Topic Preview on page 55 and the sentences you heard in the Vocabulary Preview. Write three questions that you think will be answered in the lecture. Share your questions with your classmates.

NOTETAKING PREPARATION

Showing Cause and Effect

Listen for cues that show a lecturer is expressing a cause/effect relationship between ideas. Make sure your notes reflect this relationship clearly by using the symbols below.

Cues to listen for ([C] = cause; [E] = effect)	Notes (∴ = therefore)
[C] *brings about / contributes to / results in / leads to* [E] [C] *affects / means* (*that*) */ makes / allows* [E] [C] *so* [E] [C] *therefore* [E] *As a result of* [C], [E] *Due to* [C], [E] *Because of* [C], [E]	[C] → [E] pop ↓ → oldr wrkrs ↑ [C] ∴ [E] pop ↓ ∴ oldr wrkrs ↑
[E] *because* [C] *The reason for* [E] *is* [C] [E] *is the result of* [C] [E] *is brought about by / is caused by* [C]	[E] b/c [C] oldr wrkrs ↑ b/c pop ↓ [E] ← [C] oldr wrkrs ↑ ← pop ↓

A **Look at the notes below. Match the note with the sentence. Circle *a* or *b*.**

1. Wrk chngs b/c pop chngs of wf
   a. Today, we are going to talk about a change in the world of work that has been brought about by changes in the makeup of the population of the workforce.
   b. Today, we are going to talk about a change in the world of work that has contributed to changes in the makeup of the population of the workforce.
2. Hist fac → aging of pop
   a. I will explain historical factors that are the result of the aging of the population.
   b. I will explain historical factors that have contributed to the aging of the population.
3. ↓ b'rate adv econ & + med care → ↑ lifespan ∴ older wf
   a. Two basic trends—a falling birthrate in countries with advanced economies, and improvements in medical care—have contributed to an increased lifespan, leading to an older workforce.
   b. Two basic trends—a falling birthrate in countries with advanced economies, and improvements in medical care—are the result of an increased lifespan and an older workforce.

CD 3, TR 2

B **Listen to sentences from the lecture and take notes. Use the symbols in the box to express the relationship between cause and effect.**

1. ______________________________
2. ______________________________

FIRST LISTENING

CD 3, TR 3

Listen to the lecture and number the slides on this page and the next in the order they would be shown during the lecture. Write the number of the slide on the line provided and answer the question to the right of the slide.

Elderly Support Ratio

I. Definition

II. Decline: Some statistics

III. Impact of decline

Slide #_____

What is the worldwide elderly support ratio predicted to be by 2050?

Population Changes → Graying of the Workforce

I. Population facts
   A. WHO
   B. National Institute on Aging

Slide #_____

By how much has the number of people aged 60 and over increased since 1980?

Reasons for Aging Population

I. Medical improvements

II. Changes in birthrate
   A. Industrial Revolution
   B. Start of WWII
   C. Post WWII baby boom
   D. Mid-1960s
   E. Today

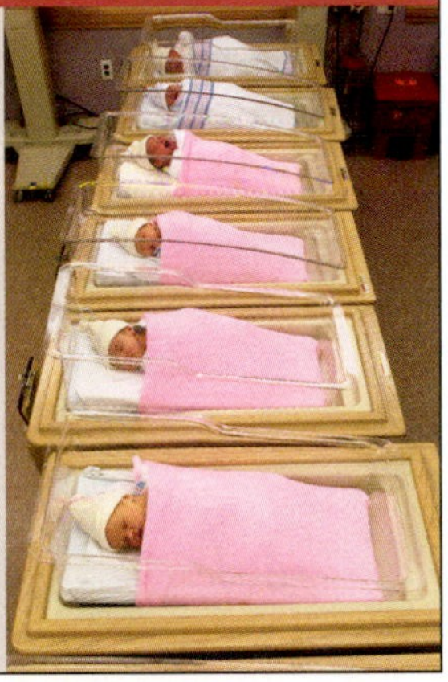

Slide #_____

Did the birthrate increase or decrease during the Industrial Revolution?

Future?

I. Longer working life

II. Workplace changes

Slide #_____

What is likely to happen in the future if the population growth rate in advanced economies remains low?

Baby Boomers

I. Continued employment

II. Retirement

Slide #_____

What does the baby boomers staying in their jobs mean for young people entering the workforce?

SECOND LISTENING

CD 3, TR 4

Now that you've listened to the lecture once, listen to it again and take notes. Write on a separate piece of paper.

THIRD LISTENING

CD 3, TR 5

You will hear parts of the lecture again. Look through your notes as you listen. A notetaking mentor will discuss the notes. Circle the answer that is closest to the notes you took, and put a check (✓) next to the notes that the mentor wrote.

Part 1

1. a.

Bef IR – lg fam adv (+) b/c
1. need cheap labor (sm farm)
2. ↑ infant mort

b.

Lg fam adv (+) ← Bef IR
1. need for cheap labor (sm farm)
2. ↑ infant mort

c.

IR ∴ lg fam adv (+) b/c
1. need for cheap labor (sm farm)
2. ↑ infant mort

Part 2

2. a.

Indus → Pop shift → need lg fam ↓
Reprod tech adv ← ctrl fam size ∴ grad ↓ in b'rate

b.

Indus → Pop shift fr rur to urb → need lg fam ↓
&
Reprod tech adv → ctrl fam size
∴
grad ↓ in b'rate

Part 3

3. a.

Am wrkr med age ↑ fr 35 (1980) to 42 (2010) →
yng wrkrs diff finding jobs

b.

BB wrk past retire age* → yng wrkrs diff finding jobs

*Stat: Am wrkr med age ↑ fr 35 (1980) to 42 (2010)

AFTER LISTENING

ACCURACY CHECK

CD 3, TR 6

You will hear questions about the lecture. Answer each question by referring to the notes that you took while listening to the lecture.

1. a. by 2015
   b. by 2050
   c. in 20 to 50 years
2. a. Large families were common.
   b. Having children cost a lot.
   c. Most people lived in cities.
3. a. high infant mortality
   b. larger families
   c. medical advances
4. a. before World War II
   b. from 1946 to 1964
   c. in the mid 1960s
5. a. China
   b. Japan
   c. South Korea
6. a. Germany
   b. Italy
   c. Japan
7. a. 14 percent
   b. 22 percent
   c. 40 percent
8. a. a shortage of workers
   b. high youth unemployment
   c. retirement of baby boomers

ORAL SUMMARY

Use your notes to create an oral summary of the lecture with your partner. As you work together, add details to your notes that your partner included but you had missed.

DISCUSSION

Discuss the following questions with a classmate or in a small group.

1. The lecturer says that we live in a youth-oriented culture. Do you agree? Is it true of your culture? If so, how might this change in the future?
2. In what ways are workplaces not suited very well to aging workers? How could workplaces be designed to accommodate the aging workforce?
3. Which would you prefer: working with people of several different generations or working with people your own age? What are the advantages and disadvantages of each?

PRE-READING

The following Reading is about a workforce trend involving young Americans. Before you read, answer the following questions. Share your answers with a classmate.

1. Look at the title. What is the workforce trend that is discussed in the article?
2. Considering what you learned in the lecture about the employment situation facing young people today, why do you think some of them would be interested in farming as a career?

READING

Now read the article.

Why Are Young, Educated Americans Going Back to the Farm?

I am a 25-year-old college graduate with a degree from a respected university, and I spend my days on my knees, hands in the dirt, pulling weeds for a living. I am a farm intern, and I am not alone. Across the country, college students and graduates like myself, many with little or no farming background, are working for almost nothing in exchange for a little instruction in running a farm.

John English, Web site manager for the National Agriculture Information Service farm internship bulletin board, said that postings there have jumped by around 500 per year for the last five years, as more small farms are established and need the cheap labor that interns provide.

Farming is difficult: There are endless chores and backbreaking physical labor. For much of the twentieth century, most Americans tried to escape such a life by moving to the city. Why would we want to go back to the farm?

The reasons are varied. Some see farming as a way to avoid participating in a capitalist economy. They share a concern for social justice and the environment, coupled with a lack of faith that existing political structures can or will deal with those issues. Other farm interns are drawn to farming by a much simpler need: paying the rent. Because of the sudden popularity of farmer's markets—that is, small markets that sell locally grown fruits, vegetables, meat, and cheese, rather

Young urban gardener with produce

than food grown thousands of miles away—a farm can look like a strong business opportunity to many young people. This is particularly true for the unemployed and those working at unfulfilling post-college jobs.

Interns interested in someday entering these growing markets must understand that when starting out they will probably earn very little. Kirk Wilson, 27, an intern at the Living Farm, earns $80 per week for his work, plus free housing and meals. Even this is more than many farms can offer. But he said he likes working outdoors and seeing things grow, and is learning the skills to run a small farm of his own someday. Having spent endless hours job hunting, Wilson also knows what he's not missing.

"I mean, am I gonna make $10 an hour for the rest of my life?" he asked. "If that's the case, then coming here and having no rent, room and board, and making $16 a day . . . I'm completely fine with that."

Increased competition for such low pay raises a potential problem, one that other attractive but low-paying fields, like journalism, are facing: Those with bills to pay or families to support, who cannot afford to accept farm wages, may be squeezed out, leaving the best farm jobs to those whose financial safety net (parents, trust fund, etc.) allows them to work for nothing.

In fact, it's likely that many of today's interns will decide to leave farming, going back to school or taking city jobs. After all, there are many obstacles to becoming a successful farmer; making a living on a small farm is as hard today as it has ever been. Government data suggests that the number of hobby farms—those earning less than $10,000 per year—increased slightly in 2010. At the same time, the number of midsized farms—those that earn between $10,000 and $100,000—decreased. And yet, the formation of groups like the National Young Farmers Coalition suggests that many small farms plan to keep going. Their goal seems less about getting rich than simply surviving, and perhaps changing a small part of the world in the process.

DISCUSSION

Discuss these questions with a classmate.

1. What surprised or interested you most about the trend described in the article? Why?
2. What information from the lecture was exemplified in the article?
3. Thinking back to what you learned from the lecture, do you agree with the author that young Americans will continue to turn to farming in the future, or is this just a temporary trend?

RESEARCH PROJECT

Individually or in a group, research one of the following topics. Write a short paper on the topic or plan and present a group presentation to inform the class about the topic.

1. A comparison of salaries by age in your country or another country in which you are interested
2. Professions that are currently facing worker shortages
3. Age discrimination
4. The growth of hobby farms in the United States

UNIT 3
VIDEO

An Actor and a Travel Writer

BEFORE VIEWING

TOPIC PREVIEW

Andrew McCarthy is both an actor and a travel writer. What are some ways that people sometimes get started in each of these careers? Compare your answers with a partner.

Started in acting	Started in travel writing

VOCABULARY PREVIEW

A **Read the definitions of these key words and phrases that you will hear during the video.**

cut from the team removed as a player from a sports team because of less skill
reticent not willing to talk very much
kicked out of college forced to leave school, usually because of bad grades or bad behavior
role a character an actor plays in a play or a movie
supported me provided me with enough money to live on
genre a particular type of writing, music, movie, etc.
encounters meetings with people that you didn't plan
scene a short event in a play or movie
my life is transitioning what I do in life is changing to something new

B **Work with a partner and discuss answers to the following questions.**

1. Have you ever been on a sports team? Have ever been **cut from the team**?
2. How would you or your family feel if you **were kicked out of college**?
3. Are you a **reticent** person? What is a topic that you are **reticent** to talk about?
4. If you had a **role** in a movie, what **genre** would you like the movie to be? What type of **scenes** would you like to be in?
5. Have you ever had an **encounter** with someone that has helped you to **transition** to a new phase of your life?
6. Who **supports** you at the moment?

VIEWING

FIRST VIEWING

Watch the video, and then compare your first impressions with a partner. Talk about what you remember, what surprised you, and what interested you.

SECOND VIEWING

Watch the video again. Listen for the missing words and write them in the blanks.

1. And so I did, and that experience, I have to say, changed my ________________.
2. And then suddenly, I got jobs very quickly, and I was suddenly a 22-year-old ________________.
3. So I started reading a lot of travel ________________, and I thought it was a very interesting genre, you know.
4. I wasn't keeping a ________________ in any way, but I would write little scenes of encounters I had with people.
5. I'll always be the ________________ who was in *Pretty in Pink*, you know?
6. So it's given me ________________ and opened ________________ for me and, you know, so it's just part of my story.

Andrew McCarthy

THIRD VIEWING

Take notes below to answer the interview questions as you watch the video. Listen for cause-and-effect cues and use indentation.

How did acting enter your life? How did you become an actor? How did you get started?

So how did travel writing enter this equation?

When you look at your life do you feel like you're more an actor or a travel writer?

AFTER VIEWING

ORAL SUMMARY

Use your notes to create an oral summary of the video with your partner. As you work together, add details to your notes that your partner included but you had missed.

DISCUSSION

Discuss the following questions with a classmate or in a small group.

1. In what ways do you think Andrew McCarthy's career as a movie star is not typical?
2. Andrew says, "At a certain point in my life, when I was about 30, I looked up and said, 'Huh?'" What do you think he means?
3. In what ways do you think your working life is or will be different from Andrew McCarthy's? In what ways do you think it might be similar?

UNIT

4

Communication

The Influence of Language, Culture, and Gender

Sticky notes with messages in the Times Square Information Center

CHAPTER

7

Classroom Communication

Language and Culture in the Classroom

TOPIC PREVIEW

Answer the following questions with a partner or your classmates.

1. What kind of communication takes place in classrooms in your culture? For example, do students talk much with each other during class time? How and when do they communicate with their teacher?
2. How do students in your culture show respect for their teachers?
3. Do you think classroom communication is the same everywhere, or is it specific to a culture? Give examples to support your answer.

Sudanese school teacher in a classroom in Nyala, Darfur

VOCABULARY PREVIEW

CD 3, TR 7

A **Read through the sentences below, which are missing vocabulary from the lecture. Listen to the sentences and write the missing words in the blanks.**

1. Communication can take the form of talk, or it can take the form of ________________, or nonverbal signals of one kind or another.
2. Many ________________ study the topic of communication in general, and speech communication specifically, in order to learn how individuals send and ________________ messages.
3. One area of research in ________________ communication is the study of the influence of the ________________, or environment, on the success or failure of communication.
4. When you are asked to picture a classroom in your ________________ eye, what do you see?
5. The "classroom" as we know it, by the way, is a relatively recent ________________.
6. In particular, culture influences the ________________ that take place in the classroom setting, and the ways that students participate in the classroom ________________.
7. Rituals are ________________ procedures used to perform a certain act or to communicate a certain message.
8. In some graduate-level seminars in American universities, students do not make any physical signs when they want to speak; they state their ideas whenever they feel the ________________.
9. North American students from families of European ________________ are usually more talkative in class and more willing to state their opinions than are students of American Indian ________________ or from Asian backgrounds.
10. The ________________ in which teachers are held also varies from culture to culture.

B **Check the spelling of the vocabulary words with your teacher. Discuss the meanings of these words and any other unfamiliar words in the sentences.**

PREDICTIONS

Think about the questions in the Topic Preview on page 68 and the sentences you heard in the Vocabulary Preview. Write three questions that you think will be answered in the lecture. Share your questions with your classmates.

NOTETAKING PREPARATION

Recording Rhetorical Questions

In a lecture, the main points are often introduced as *rhetorical questions*. A rhetorical question is a question that the speaker does not expect the listener to answer. The question is a way to call attention to a main point that the lecturer will go on to develop.

Here are some examples of cues frequently used for rhetorical questions and their answers.

When . . . what do you . . . ? You probably . . .	Just what (exactly) is/are . . . ? The definition of . . .
But what do we mean by . . . ? Basically, . . .	And what about . . . ? Well, . . .

When you hear a rhetorical question in a lecture, be sure to record it. Use a simple abbreviation to label the question and answer.

Q = rhetorical question   A = answer

Put the question above the answer and use indentation to show the details, support, or explanation—in other words, the answer to the question. For example:

Lecture

But what do we mean by culture? Basically, culture provides us with a system of knowledge that allows us to communicate with others and teaches us how to interpret their verbal and nonverbal behavior.

Notes

Q: Wht is cult
A: syst knowl for
- comm ↔ others
- interp vb & nonvb behv

A **Rewrite the notes using the abbreviations *Q* and *A* and indentation.**

But wh ex is a clssrm? Ans influ by cult & incl teach/stud rel, how info tght and lrnd, how teach/stud comm

CD 3, TR 8

B **Listen to a part of the lecture and complete the notes. A heading has been provided. Remember to use *Q* and *A* and indentation.**

Lang, cult, and comm in clssrms

FIRST LISTENING

CD 3, TR 9

Listen to the lecture and number the slides on this page and the next in the order they would be shown during the lecture. Write the number of the slide on the line provided and answer the question to the right of the slide.

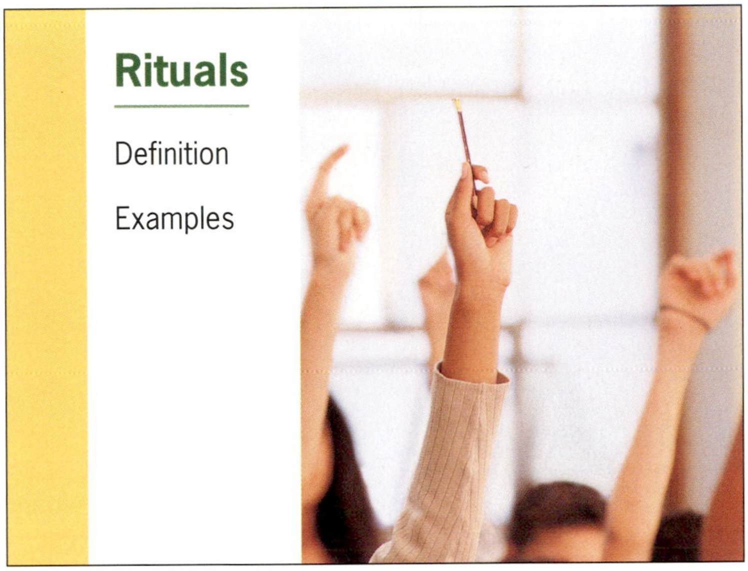

Slide #_____

How do Jamaican students signal that they want to answer a question?

Slide #_____

What influences the image that people have of a classroom?

Language, Culture, and Communication

Definition of communication

Verbal and nonverbal

Intercultural communication

- Setting

Slide #_____

How do people communicate their thoughts, feelings, and intentions to others?

Treatment of Teachers

Asia

Germany

Israel

Slide #_____

In which country or region do students sometimes criticize their teachers in class?

Classroom Participation

European American

American Indian

Asian

Slide #_____

Which North American students are the more talkative in class?

SECOND LISTENING

CD 3, TR 10

Now that you have listened to the lecture once, listen to it again and take notes. Write on a separate piece of paper.

THIRD LISTENING

CD 3, TR 11

You will hear parts of the lecture again. Look through your notes as you listen. A notetaking mentor will discuss the notes. Circle the answer that is closest to the notes you took, and put a check (✓) next to the notes that the mentor wrote.

Part 1

1. a.

Q: Wht is cult?
A: Sys of know that...
- allows comm w/ others
- teaches how to intrprt ppl's v and nv beh
- influ how ppl interact

b.

Q: Wht is cult?
A: Term usd in diff ways
- sys of know that allows comm w/ others
- teaches how to intrprt ppl's v and nv beh
- influ how ppl interact

c.

Q: What do we mean by culture?
A: Basic – cult provide syst of know that allows us to comm w/ others and teaches us how to interpret their verb and nonverb behav – influences how ppl interact

Part 2

2. a.

Q: Wht r rituals?
A: Sys proc
↙ ↘
prfrm act comm msg

b.

Dictionary def of rituals = syst proc to prfrm act or comm msg. Many rits in ed. T enters clssrm, st stand up

c.

Q: Wht r rituals?
A: Syst proced to prfrm act or comm msg many in educ
ex: T enters clssrm, st stand up

Part 3

3. a.

Q: How much r Ts respctd?
A: Varies fr cult to cult
- Asns – Ts sym of learn & cult
- Ger – value T's opin so don't disagr w/ T in clss
- Israel – can critic T

b.

Q: How r Ts treated? How much r they respctd?
A: Varies – Asns – Ts respctd – symbol of learn & cult Ger – don't disagr in clss Israel – can critic T

AFTER LISTENING

ACCURACY CHECK

CD 3, TR 12

You will hear questions about the lecture. Answer each question by referring to the notes that you took while listening to the lecture.

1. a. system of knowledge
   b. expected communication procedures
   c. a form of human behavior

2. a. a classroom ritual
   b. cross-cultural communication
   c. speech communication

3. a. being talkative in class
   b. correcting a teacher
   c. finger snapping

4. a. exchange ideas with classmates
   b. explore issues for themselves
   c. speak only if the teacher speaks to them

5. a. The teacher is a symbol of learning.
   b. Teachers give their opinions.
   c. Teachers are criticized.

6. a. Criticizing a teacher is acceptable.
   b. Contradicting a teacher is considered rude.
   c. It is acceptable to correct a teacher.

7. a. Asians and American Indians
   b. European Americans and Germans
   c. Americans and Israelis

8. a. student-teacher classroom interaction
   b. relationships outside of class
   c. nonverbal communication

ORAL SUMMARY

Use your notes to create an oral summary of the lecture with your partner. As you work together, add details to your notes that your partner included but you had missed.

DISCUSSION

Discuss the following questions with a classmate or in a small group.

1. The lecturer says that teachers in some cultures are honored members of society. Is this true in your culture? If so, how is this esteem demonstrated? If not, how are teachers seen in your culture?
2. What are some classroom rituals in your culture that were not mentioned in the lecture? Are they similar to those in other cultures with which you are familiar?
3. The classroom rituals discussed in the lecture were mostly nonverbal. Can you think of any verbal classroom rituals?

EXPANSION

PRE-READING

The following Reading is about communicating in a third language. Before you read, answer the following questions. Share your answers with a classmate.

1. Look at the title of the article. What is a *lingua franca*? Based on the title and the photograph, what do you think the article will be about?
2. Do you think that your personality changes when you speak English? Discuss any changes you have noticed and talk about what the reasons might be.

READING

Now read the article.

Love that Lingua Franca

Michiko, the young Japanese woman I'm sharing a seat with on a bus near Tokyo, speaks a shy, hesitant English. I resign myself to a couple of hours filled with awkward, polite English. But then something unexpected happens. Grasping for a subject to talk about with her, I spot the headline on the cover of a local tourism brochure, written in Japanese and English. Japanese has Chinese characters in its writing system and I can read Chinese, so I immediately notice that the characters for the Japanese word "*Chiba*" mean "One Thousand Leaves."

Pointing to the brochure, I turn to Michiko and say: "*Chiba* means one thousand leaves."

"Yes!" she responds, then adds in a French accent that is much better than mine, "*Milles feuilles*—A thousand leaves." "*Mais alors*—So," I say, "*vous parlez français*—you speak French." "No," she answers, and, once again in a perfect accent, says "*Hablo español*—I speak Spanish." Fantastic! "*Yo también*—me, too," I tell her. We've found common ground, and race into an extended conversation.

As shy as Michiko is in English, she's confident and funny when she speaks in Spanish. It has been observed that we often change personalities when we switch languages. I don't speak any Japanese, so I don't know what Michiko is like in her mother tongue. In the third tongue of Spanish, however, we blast past not just linguistic but cultural differences to have a real conversation.

This isn't the first time I've experienced the thrill of connecting with someone in a third-party tongue, which is what I call a common language that's nonnative to both speakers. Since I believe every traveler should speak other languages, I have spent years learning two myself, Spanish and Cantonese. When I'm in Madrid or Guangzhou, I do my best to keep up with the rapid, slangy conversation of native speakers. I lean forward into the conversations and listen with all my concentration and heart, but after a while of struggling I become exhausted and frustrated, and soon give up.

The not-native-to-either-party language is like a neutral territory, a halfway point where the joys and difficulties of communication are shared equally. I speak more slowly, knowing that my listeners may not "hear" me like a native; they do the same. As a traveler, I want my words to bring me closer to people, so I grab every chance I get to use that most democratic and liberating language of all, the third tongue. Sometimes just finding a third tongue can be an adventure. One day in India's northern state of Rajasthan, I suddenly heard a very familiar rhythm of sounds. I turned and found four European women discussing the architectural details of a temple in Spanish. I greeted them with an "*¡Hola!*" and we ended up having lunch together.

Cenotaph tombs in India

Back in the bus with Michiko, we finally arrive at our destination. We fall out of Spanish and back into our mother languages and our roles: the local person and the foreign tourist. Now, though, we know the third tongue will be there when we need it.

DISCUSSION

Discuss the following questions with a classmate or in a small group.

1. In what ways does the information in the article provide support for the ideas introduced in the lecture regarding cross-cultural communication?
2. Does anything in the article refute the ideas introduced in the lecture? If so, what? Be specific.
3. The article addresses the advantages of communicating in a third tongue. Using what you have learned from the lecture, discuss the possible disadvantages.

RESEARCH PROJECT

Individually or in a group, research one of the following topics. Write a short paper on the topic, or plan and present a presentation to inform the class about the topic.

1. Classroom communication patterns in your culture or in another culture in which you have an interest
2. Nonverbal communication in your culture as compared to another culture in which you have an interest
3. A comparison of business communication patterns in two cultures
4. Another related topic that interests you or your group

CHAPTER

8

Gender and Communication

Male–Female Conversation as Cross-cultural Communication

TOPIC PREVIEW

Answer the following questions with a partner or your classmates.

1. In your culture, what kinds of games do little girls play? Do little boys play the same kinds of games? If not, how are the games of boys and girls different?
2. Look at the title of the chapter. Is male–female communication a type of cross-cultural communication? Explain.
3. In your culture, is there a difference in the way that men and women communicate in different situations, for example, in a business meeting, at a party, in a class seminar or small class, at a family dinner? Explain your answers.

BEFORE LISTENING

VOCABULARY PREVIEW

CD 3, TR 13

A **Read through the sentences below, which are missing vocabulary from the lecture. Listen to the sentences and write the missing words in the blanks.**

1. Boys learn to be _________________ and girls learn to be _________________ as they grow to be men and women.
2. Children learn how to talk to other children or adults, and how to have conversations, not only from their parents, but also from their _________________.
3. Deborah Tannen and other researchers on this topic have found that young boys tend to play outside the home rather than in, and they play in large groups that are _________________ structured.
4. It is by giving orders and making the other boys play by the rules that boys achieve higher and more _________________ status in the play group.
5. Boys also achieve _________________ by taking center _________________.
6. The boys were making slingshots; the girls were making _________________.
7. The girls making the rings were more _________________.
8. As a result of our cultural _________________, we learn norms of behavior and patterns of communication that are often gender based, and sometimes gender _________________.
9. Well, perhaps it is our social concept of what is feminine and what is masculine that reinforces the _________________ that women talk more than men, and even causes these different patterns of communication.
10. This means that a Zulu wife must _________________ and find other ways to say these things.

B **Check the spelling of the vocabulary words with your teacher. Discuss the meanings of these words and any other unfamiliar words in the sentences.**

PREDICTIONS

Think about the questions in the Topic Preview on page 77 and the sentences you heard in the Vocabulary Preview. Write three questions that you think will be answered in the lecture. Share your questions with your classmates.

NOTETAKING PREPARATION

Contrast Cues and Charts

Listen for cues that show a lecturer is expressing a contrast, or difference, between two things. Make sure your notes reflect this relationship clearly by using the symbols below.

Cues to listen for	Notes
different / differently / difference	≠ DIFF
less / fewer (than) / not as . . . as	$<$ — ↓
-er / more (than)	$>$ + ↑
on the other hand/however	↓ BUT
the (exact) opposite	≠

A chart with side-by-side lists helps make contrasts clear. You can organize your notes in a chart after the lecture. Use symbols for contrasts and indents for main ideas and supporting details.

Boys: lrg grps outside, ↑ hierarch-leader-ordrs ≠ Girls: sm grps or 2s, ↓ hierarch. Ex: hopsc, jump rp, take turn-suggs not ordr

Girls	Boys
• sm grps or 2s	• lrg grps
• ↓ hierarch = take turn, suggs Ex: hopsc, jump rp	• ↑ hierarch = leader, ordrs
	• + outside

Use the same order in each column. If something is mentioned for only one of the things being compared, put that point at the end.

A **On a separate piece of paper, reorganize the notes in the chart below to show comparisons in the same order, side-by-side.**

Boys	Girls
• + talk -joke, story	Games – no win/losers
• + ordrs	
• dom conv—interr	Comm Styls
Games	• ↓ dir ordrs
• win/losers	• ↑ suggs
• + rules	

CD 3, TR 14

B **Listen to a part of the lecture for the notes below. Rewrite the notes as a chart.**

Rsrch: MH Goodwin—comp boys/girls task. Boys=make slshot/Girls=jewlry/ Boys-hierarch/lder tld what & how ≠ Girls-egal-ev suggs; list & accpt sugg

FIRST LISTENING

CD 3, TR 15

Listen to the lecture and number the slides on this page and the next in the order they would be shown during the lecture. Write the number of the slide on the line provided and answer the question to the right of the slide.

Social Concepts Reinforce Stereotyping

Feminine/Masculine behavior

Example from Zulu culture

Slide #____

What are women taught about how to be feminine?

Learning to Communicate Through Play

Boys' play
- large groups
- hierarchy

Girls' play
- small groups
- take turns

Slide #____

How do boys achieve status when playing?

Slide #_____

Are the stereotypes about how much women talk accurate?

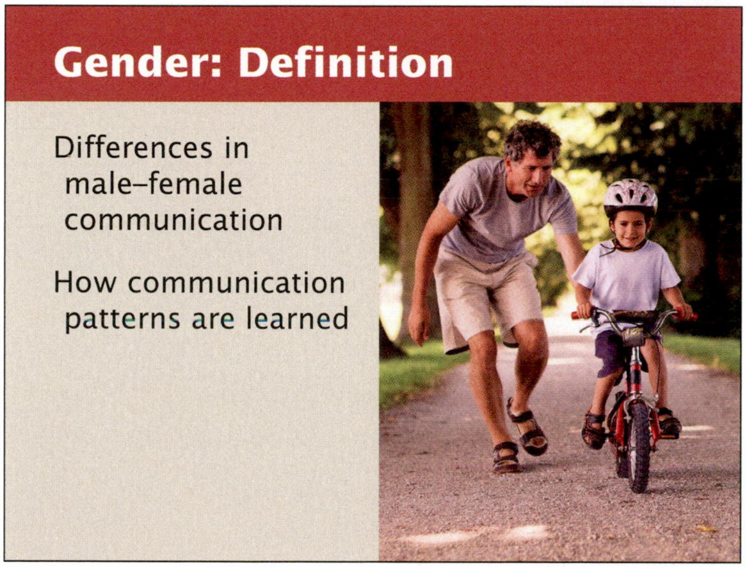

Slide #_____

How are communication patterns learned?

Slide #_____

What was the main finding of the Eakins' study?

SECOND LISTENING

CD 3, TR 16

Now that you've listened to the lecture once, listen to it again and take notes. Write on a separate piece of paper.

THIRD LISTENING

CD 3, TR 17

You will hear parts of the lecture again. Look through your notes as you listen. A notetaking mentor will discuss the notes. Circle the answer that is closest to the notes you took, and put a check (✓) next to the notes that the mentor wrote.

Part 1

1. a.

who tlks & intrpt more?
stereotype = women > men
BUT
reality = men > women

b.

The stereotype is woman take center stage by talking & interrupt but research show opposite is true

c.

Men	Women
talk & intrpt <women	talk & intrpt <men
(stereo)	(true)

Part 2

2. a.

Male profs	F'male profs
Res #1 (Eakins) 7 univ fac mtgs	Res #1
• talkd 10.66–17.07 sec	• talkd 3–10 sec
Res #2 (Simeone) univ dept mtgs	Res #2
• 46% said they talkd	• 15% said they talked

b.

Res #1	Res #2
Eakins	Simeone
7 univ fac mtgs; timed who talked	univ dept mtgs – who said they talkd?
male prof: 10.66–17.07 sec	male prof: 46%
f'male " : 3–10 sec	f'male " : 15%

Part 3

3. a.

Men	Women
cult says tlking/intrpt ok	cult says tlking/intrpt NOT ok
not critic for tlking/intrpt	critic for tlking/intrpt, even if just a little

b.

Cult Expec

Masculine role	Feminine role
expected = ↑ talk & intrpt	expected = ↓ talk & intrpt
SO	SO
↓ critic, even if they do it ↑	↑ critic, even if they do it ↓

AFTER LISTENING

ACCURACY CHECK

CD 3, TR 18

You will hear questions about the lecture. Answer each question by referring to the notes that you took while listening to the lecture.

1. a. from conversations
   b. from brothers and sisters
   c. from parents and other children
2. a. They play together a lot.
   b. They prefer same-sex groups.
   c. They rarely play together.
3. a. Girls are less hierarchical.
   b. Girls don't care who wins.
   c. Girls enjoy team sports more.
4. a. Girls suggest, but boys order.
   b. Girls talk more.
   c. Boys argue more.
5. a. to make others laugh
   b. to make friends
   c. to achieve status
6. a. a little girl playing hopscotch
   b. a little boy making a slingshot
   c. a little boy or girl playing house
7. a. Women are encouraged to talk.
   b. Men talk and interrupt more.
   c. Women talk and interrupt more.
8. a. family relationships
   b. gender in communication
   c. an unequal society

ORAL SUMMARY

Use your notes to create an oral summary of the lecture with your partner. As you work together, add details to your notes that your partner included but you had missed.

DISCUSSION

Discuss the following questions with a classmate or in a small group.

1. What stereotypes do you have in your culture about how women communicate? About men? Do you think these stereotypes are an accurate description of male and female communication patterns? Why or why not?
2. What are some of the differences in the ways that women and men communicate in your culture?
3. Based on what was said in the lecture, do you think that Deborah Tannen would support single-sex education—that is, having all-boy and all-girl schools? Why or why not?
4. In your culture, are single-sex schools common? Would you prefer your children to be educated in a single-sex school, or a mixed-sex one? Why?

PRE-READING

The following Reading is about a study on group intelligence. Before you read, answer the following questions. Share your answers with a classmate.

1. Look at the title of the article. Write two things that you expect to learn from the article.
2. Based on what you learned in the lecture, do you think groups with more female than male members would be better at thought-based tasks such as visual puzzles?

READING

Now read the article.

Smarter Teams Are More Sensitive, Have More Women?

Being smart doesn't matter much if you're working in a group, according to the first study to calculate collective intelligence—a group's ability to succeed at a variety of tasks.

Surprisingly, in a team an individual's intelligence has little to do with success in thought-based tasks such as visual puzzles and negotiating over limited resources, a set of recent experiments found. Instead, a group is more successful if it contains people who are more "socially sensitive"—in this case meaning they're better able to read emotions from people's faces.

That also explains why groups with more women—who score higher on tests of social sensitivity—were more likely to excel, said study leader Anita Williams Woolley, an expert in collective intelligence at Carnegie Mellon University in Pittsburgh. Particularly intelligent groups also had more people who took turns speaking, according to the study, published in the journal *Science*. "There's such a focus on individual intelligence and individual accomplishment, especially in western culture," she said. "As our world becomes flatter and more interconnected, it's not as important to consider what an individual can do by themselves but what they can do collectively."

Calculating Collective Intelligence

Individual intelligence is measured by the ability of a person to do multiple tasks well, Woolley said. To see if the same would be true of groups, Woolley and

colleagues recruited 699 volunteers and first measured each person's intelligence and social sensitivity using standard psychological tests.

The volunteers were then split into groups of two to five and asked to do some simple tasks, such as solving a visual puzzle. The results revealed that certain groups were better at all types of tasks, which is the "primary evidence for the notion of collective intelligence," Woolley said. Next, the groups were each asked to perform more complex tasks, which included playing a video game against an imaginary opponent and solving a research-and-development problem. As suspected, the groups' collective intelligence scores from the first round of tests predicted how they'd do on the complex experiments, Woolley said.

Findings May Benefit Real-World Groups

This ability to predict group success may offer guidance in real-life situations—especially as more decisions in fields such as business and the military are made in consensus-based settings, she said. For instance, knowing a group's collective intelligence could be vital in a high-risk situation where poor performance could mean failure, such as starting a new business.

Group Smarts Rooted in Animal Kingdom

Group intelligence may also be rooted in the past. For instance, "You can't be really good at hunting but not good at gathering," Woolley said. "Figuring out how to more flexibly deploy the skills available through members of groups would be associated with survival."

Likewise, Woolley said, the study is evidence that human societies may function better in groups. "It's no mistake that some of the earlier work on collective intelligence does borrow from the animal kingdom." For instance, "ants are simple creatures but collectively can accomplish things that are amazing."

DISCUSSION

Discuss these questions with a classmate.

1. How does the information in the article provide support for the ideas introduced in the lecture regarding male–female patterns of communication?
2. Did anything in the article surprise you because it seemed different from what you heard in the lecture? If so, what? Be specific.
3. The study's findings seem to suggest that strong communication skills, both verbal and nonverbal, are related to intelligence. Based on what you have learned from the lecture, why do you think that might be true?

RESEARCH PROJECT

Individually or in a group, research one of the following topics. Write a short paper on the topic, or plan and present a group presentation to inform the class about the topic.

1. The role of communication in collective intelligence (also known as *swarm intelligence*)
2. Male and female communication patterns in Zulu culture
3. Classroom communication in your culture or in another culture in which you have an interest
4. Another related topic that interests you or your group

UNIT 4
VIDEO
Digital Nomad

BEFORE VIEWING

TOPIC PREVIEW

Twitter is a form of communication in which people write short messages, called *Tweets*. Answer these questions about Tweets with a partner.

1. What do you know about Tweets, and how to write them?
2. Do you have a Twitter account? If so, what do you Tweet about?
3. Can you name any famous people who Tweet? What sorts of things do they Tweet about?
4. Do you think Tweeting is easy, fun, or silly? Why or why not?

VOCABULARY PREVIEW

A **Read the definitions of these vocabulary words and phrases that you will hear during the video.**

a real-time narrative a story told at the same time that an event is happening
memoir a written story of the events in someone's life
a pro a person with professional skill at doing something
tips pieces of useful advice
eclipse cover or block something that is more important
a wildebeest carcass the dead body of a large African animal with curving horns, also called a *gnu*
there was no reception cell phones couldn't operate because there was no signal
obsessed thinking about only one particular thing and not anything else
unplug periodically to take a break from using electronic devices sometimes

B **Work with a partner and write in the blank the word from the box that best completes the sentence.**

event	record	river	Tweets
explorers	remember	technology	video

1. The early ________________ wrote **memoirs**, but modern writers like to write **real-time narratives**.
2. It is difficult to be **a pro** at writing ________________.
3. There was **no reception** anywhere, except for one place, which was down by the ________________, next to a **wildebeest carcass**.
4. It's possible to use modern ________________ too much. Let me give you an important **tip**: ________________ to **unplug periodically**.
5. Don't become so **obsessed** with trying to ________________ an experience by writing or shooting ________________ that you allow your obsession to **eclipse** your ability to experience the ________________.

VIEWING

FIRST VIEWING

Watch the video, and then compare your first impressions with a partner. Talk about what you remember, what surprised you, and what interested you.

SECOND VIEWING

Watch the video again. Listen for the missing words and write them in the blanks.

1. Now this follows an ancient ________________ form of poetry. But it's very short and it has all the great ingredients of a Tweet, of ________________.
2. And I've Tweeted—not underwater, that doesn't work yet, but almost. I Tweeted in ________________ time while flying a plane, in French.
3. And they always wanted to drive by the carcass, because the carcass for whatever ________________ had coverage. So they could always ________________ their e-mail and their Tweets whenever we got by the carcass.
4. We take much better pictures than ________________ do. We feel a place. We have these ________________.

A wildebeest

THIRD VIEWING

Complete these notes as you watch the video. Use abbreviations and symbols as necessary.

Use Twitter
- orig NG explorers – keep jurnl, wrt bk later = ______________ mem
- A.E. – real time mem, ______________

Lrning to Tweet (sent 5000 fr DC to Antarctica)
- Twitter = short ______________ = 140 ______________
- lrnd fr ______________, eg Haiku (Jap) is ______________
- set stage
- ______________
- place
- ______________
- character
- ______________

Tips
1. be there
2. shar'g must not ______________
   - EX journalists w
     - miss beauty & ______________
     - no phone recp – 1 spot; obsessed & ______________
3. if obsessed w ______________ you ______________
4. unplug, because ______________

AFTER VIEWING

ORAL SUMMARY

Use your notes to create an oral summary of the video with your partner. As you work together, add details to your notes that your partner included but you had missed.

DISCUSSION

Discuss the following questions with a classmate or in a small group.

1. How is Andrew Evans similar to the first National Geographic explorers? How is he different?
2. Write a Tweet. Use Andrew's tips for writing a good Tweet. Remember, you can only use 140 characters or less.
3. What are Andrew Evans' tips for being a good digital nomad? Do you agree that people need to "unplug"? Why or why not?
4. Andrew says, "Never let sharing the experience eclipse having the experience." What does he mean? Do you think this is a problem? Give examples.

UNIT 5

Biology

From Genetics to Genetic Engineering

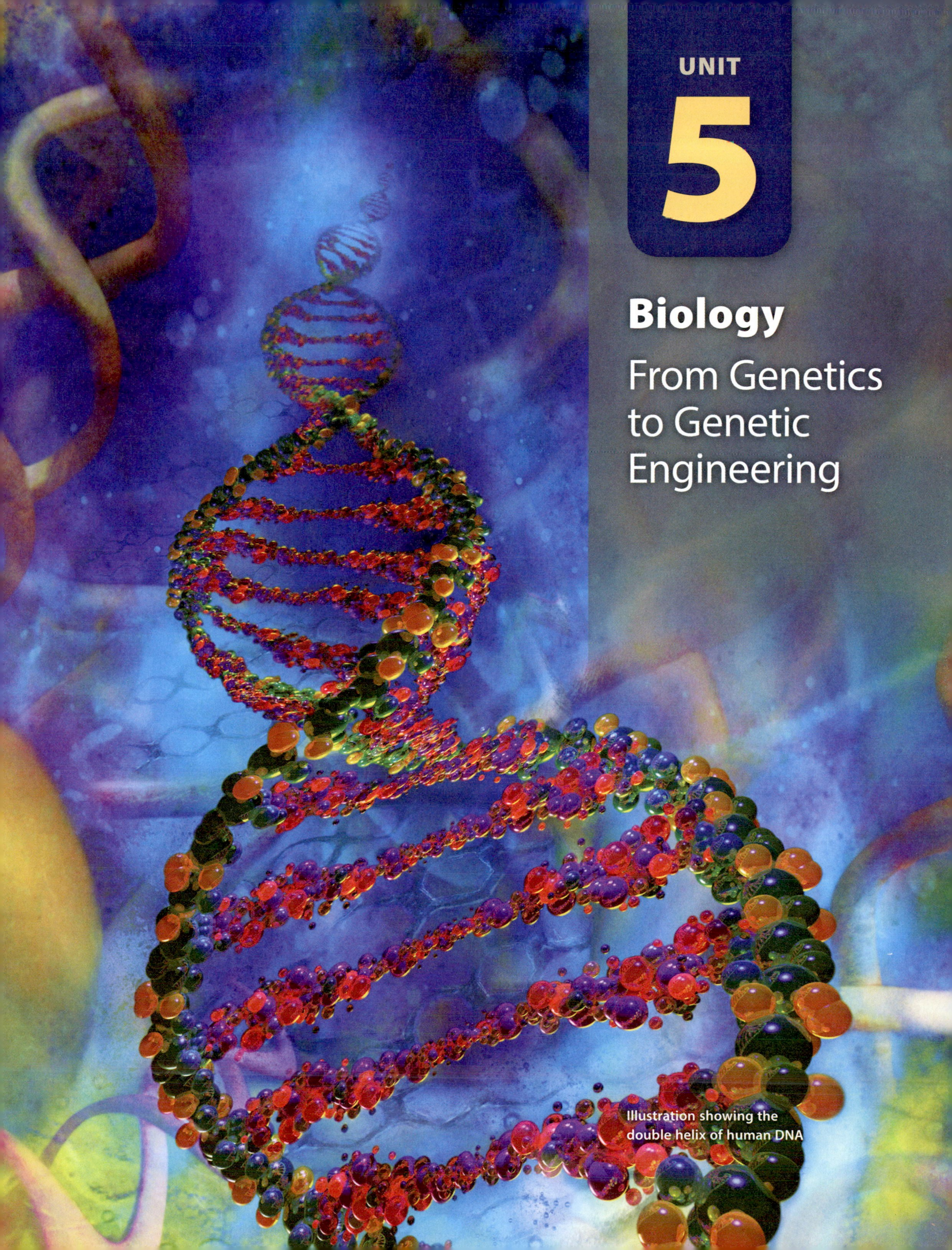

Illustration showing the double helix of human DNA

CHAPTER

9

The Origins of Genetics

Mendel and the Garden Pea Experiment

TOPIC PREVIEW

Answer the following questions with a partner or your classmates.

1. Why do people look the way they do? Why do you look similar to, but different from, your parents, brothers, and sisters?
2. Look at the title of this chapter. Can you guess who Mendel was and how his study of pea plants furthered our understanding of heredity and genetics?
3. How can an understanding of genetics help agriculture?

Gregor Mendel

BEFORE LISTENING

VOCABULARY PREVIEW

CD 4, TR 1

A **Read through the sentences below, which are missing vocabulary from the lecture. Listen to the sentences and write the missing words in the blanks.**

1. ________________ determine how every living creature on earth appears, how it functions, how it ________________, and generally, how it behaves.
2. Inherited ________________, or characteristics, are determined by ________________ of genes that are different for every human being.
3. The scientists who study how genes are ________________ and passed from one generation to the next are called ________________.
4. I want to ________________ and briefly examine the work of a ________________ in biology, Gregor Mendel.
5. Mendel studied science at the University of Vienna, and there he learned how to use mathematics to try to explain natural ________________.
6. When a variety of garden pea that had violet flowers was ________________ with a variety that had white flowers, all the ________________ surprisingly had only violet flowers.
7. Mendel applied his knowledge of mathematics and statistics to help him ________________ the results of the ________________ of the white-flowering and violet-flowering plants.
8. The pea plants could be ________________ quickly, and with little effort.
9. We now know that genes are tiny ________________ structures inside each cell that determine eye color, blood type, height, and so on.
10. A person may have a genetic ________________ toward being overweight, but the person's actual weight will depend on a number of environmental ________________.

B **Check the spelling of the vocabulary words with your teacher. Discuss the meanings of these words and any other unfamiliar words in the sentences.**

PREDICTIONS

Think about the questions in the Topic Preview on page 90 and the sentences you heard in the Vocabulary Preview. Write three questions that you think will be answered in the lecture. Share your questions with your classmates.

NOTETAKING PREPARATION

Anticipating and Recording Examples

In the course of a lecture, you will almost always hear examples that explain or reinforce an important point. Here is some language a lecturer might use to introduce an example:

For example, . . . *. . . like . . .* *Let me give you an example. . . .*
. . . including . . . *. . . such as . . .*

When you hear a lecturer use any of these phrases, use one of the following abbreviations in your notes to show you are recording an example:

EX – For ex – e.g. –

Remember that examples support a main point.

- List them under the related main point in your notes.
- Indent them to show that they are less important than the main point.
- Leave extra room so that you can later add examples or details you may have missed.

A **Look at the lecture notes below. With a partner, read the notes out loud as sentences. Think of some possible examples the lecturer might give. Write them on a separate paper.**

1. Genes—passed dn – gener → gener – e.g. . . .

2. Many traits ≈ prnts' trts, e.g. . . .

3. We breed anmls to be better—For ex racehorse: > . . .

4. Garden pea: many traits w/ 2 diff forms – e.g. . . .

5. Pers cn hv genet tend to ovrwt, BUT also dep on environ: EX . . .

CD 4, TR 2

B **Listen to the sentences from the lecture for the notes in A above. Write the examples that you hear in the space under the notes. Remember to indent. Compare the examples you heard with those you wrote on a separate paper. Were some of your predictions in A correct?**

FIRST LISTENING

CD 4, TR 3

Listen to the lecture and number the slides on this page and the next in the order they would be shown during the lecture. Write the number of the slide on the line provided and answer the question to the right of the slide.

The Garden Pea Experiments

Thomas Knight
- Unexplained results

Gregor Mendel
- Repeated Knight
- Applied statistical analysis

Advantages of pea plant

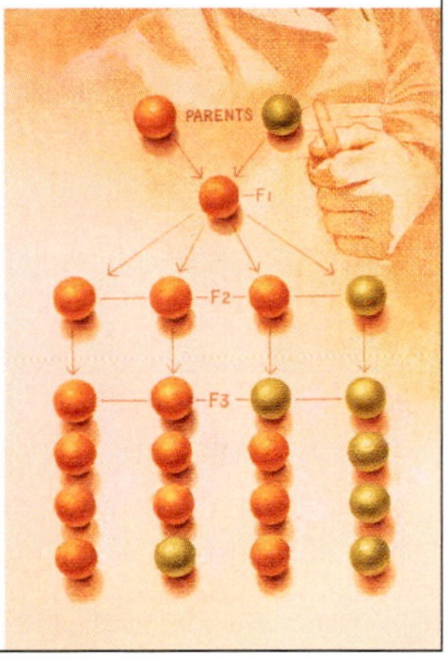

Slide #_____

What is one reason why Mendel used pea plants in his experiments?

available
cultivated
produce more

What Are Genes?

What genes do

DNA

Genes are inherited

Field of study

Slide #_____

What do genes determine?

Genetics Today

What we learned from Mendel

Genes and heredity

Nongenetic factors that influence who we are

Slide #____

Do we understand genetics and heredity completely today?

Gregor Mendel (1822–1884)

Early experiments with pea plants

Monestary

- Teacher 1840
- Study at University of Vienna 1851

1853

Slide #____

How are Mendel's principles referred to today?

Interest in How Heredity Works

Examples

- Crops
- Animals

Slide #____

What example does the lecturer use to illustrate how heredity works in an animal?

CD 4, TR 4

SECOND LISTENING

Now that you have listened to the lecture once, listen to it again and take notes. Write on a separate piece of paper.

CD 4, TR 5

THIRD LISTENING

You will hear parts of the lecture again. Look through your notes as you listen. A notetaking mentor will discuss the notes. Circle the answer that is closest to the notes you took, and put a check (✓) next to the notes that the mentor wrote.

Part 1

1. a.

Gs
- in bd cells
- md of DNA (=instrs for Gs)
- inher'd
  EX – hair col

b.

Gs fnd in cells of bod
md of deoksy___ ?
instrs each cell supposd... ?
Gs passd dn
inher int trts frm grmoth/fath

Part 2

2. a.

Mendel –intr – see rl man
1843 became monk
1851 – Univ Vien
math & exper biol
2 yrs – left un.
- nrvs tak exam
- bcm famous sci

b.

Mendel
1842 monk – teach
1851 Univ Vien – math & biol

c.

Mendel

Part 3

3. a.

Tm Knight – pea flwr exp:
viol fl X wh. fl = all v offspr (!)
BUT v X v offspr = v & w (!)
– w reapp – K cdnt expl

b.

Tm Knight exp w/viol & wh pea flwrs
(v) X (w)
↓
1. all (v) (!)
BUT 1. (v) X (v)
↓
2. both (v) & (w) (!?– K)

AFTER LISTENING

ACCURACY CHECK

CD 4, TR 6

You will hear questions about the lecture. Answer each question by referring to the notes that you took while listening to the lecture.

1. a. our DNA
   b. how living creatures function
   c. everything about us

2. a. They are identical.
   b. They are unique to each person.
   c. Most are the same in all people.

3. a. They are completely different.
   b. Many are the same.
   c. They are 97 percent the same.

4. a. more than 200 years old
   b. less than 40 years old
   c. less than 200 years old

5. a. mathematics
   b. biology
   c. both a and b

6. a. Their inherited traits are predictable.
   b. They are always either violet or white.
   c. They reproduce very quickly.

7. a. to breed stronger animals
   b. to win races
   c. to grow wheat instead of corn

8. a. body weight
   b. eye color
   c. height

ORAL SUMMARY

Use your notes to create an oral summary of the lecture with a partner. As you work together, add details to your notes that your partner included but you had missed.

DISCUSSION

Discuss the following questions with a classmate or in a small group.

1. What evidence do you see for heredity in your family? Discuss physical and behavioral or intellectual traits.
2. The lecturer described Thomas Knight's experiments crossing plants with violet and white flowers, and pointed out his confusion when the white flowers reappeared in the second generation. Can you or any of your classmates explain why this happened? Review the experiment and discuss.
3. The lecturer states that most of what we know today about genetics has been learned in the past few decades. Why do you think this is true?

EXPANSION

PRE-READING

The following Reading is about how genetic patterns can be traced through human history. Before you read, answer the following questions. Share your answers with a classmate.

1. Look at the picture of a cell below. Can you identify the different parts of the cell? Where are the genes?
2. Scan the article and locate the two subtitles. For each subtitle, write a question that you would like to have answered.

READING

Now read the article.

Genes and Population Genetics

The human body is made of some 50 to 100 trillion cells, which form the basic units of life and combine to form more complex tissues and organs. Inside each cell, genes comprise a "blueprint" for protein production that determines how the cell will function. Genes also determine physical traits. The complete set of some 20,000 to 25,000 genes is called the genome. Only a tiny fraction of the total genome sets the human body apart from those of other animals.

Most cells have similar basic structure. An outer layer, called the cell membrane, contains fluid called cytoplasm. Within the cytoplasm are many different specialized "little organs," called organelles. The most important of these is the nucleus, which controls the cell and houses the genetic material in structures called chromosomes. Another type of organelle is the mitochondria. These "cellular power plants" have their own genome, and do not recombine during reproduction.

During reproduction, each cell's DNA, which is in the form of a double helix, separates into two unique strands. The individual strands duplicate themselves for the next generation, but the process is not always perfect. Random "copying errors," or mutations, can and do occur along the genome's long spelling sequence of base pairs.

When mutations are passed down through the generations they become genetic markers of descent, forming a complex story that can be traced backward in time. The exact shape of this tree is also affected by natural selection and migration.

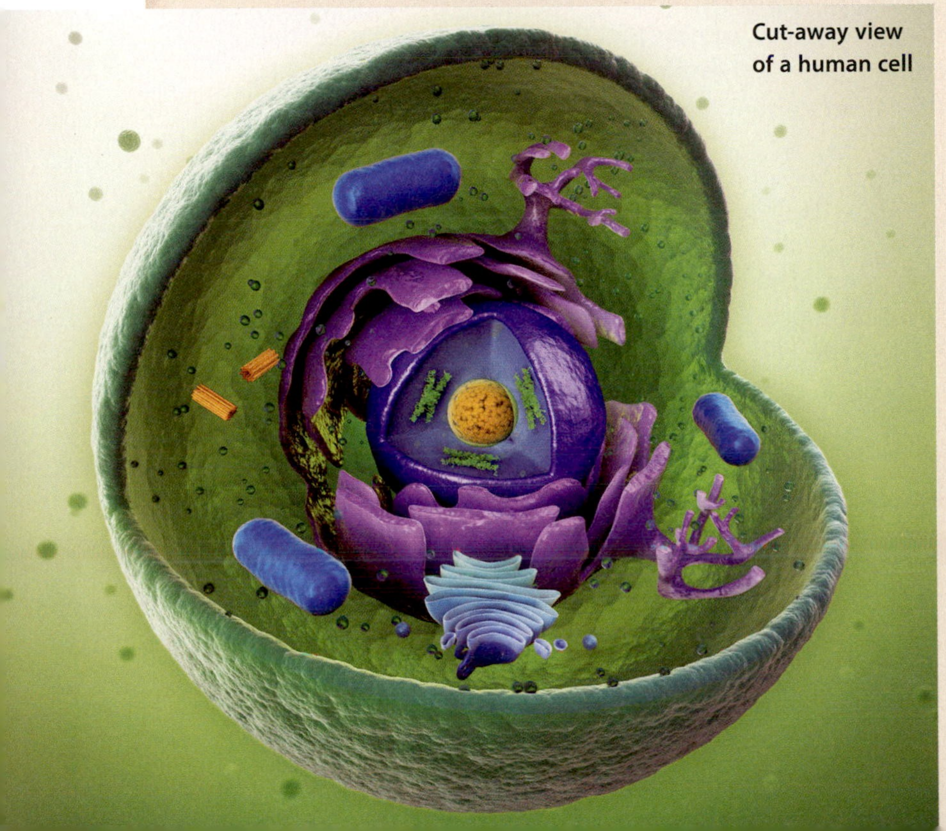

Cut-away view of a human cell

Natural selection

Natural selection is a process that favors beneficial genetic mutations and limits harmful ones. Organisms that possess an advantageous trait either attract mates more easily or survive in greater numbers. Such traits are passed on to increasingly larger numbers of individuals with each successive generation. The cumulative effect of natural selection produces populations that have evolved to succeed in their unique environments. This effect is readily seen in the physical diversity of plants, animal species, and human populations worldwide.

Migration

Y-chromosome DNA, passed from father to son, and mitochondrial DNA, passed from a mother to all her children, are varied through the generations only by occasional natural mutations, or genetic markers. These mutations, occurring in an otherwise continuous string of genetic replication, serve as genetic signposts for tracing human evolution. By following a marker back though time to its origin, geneticists can identify the most recent common ancestor of everyone alive who carries a given marker. The divergent branches of the human family tree, represented by groups carrying a particular genetic marker, can be followed back to "nodes" on the tree where a mutation split a branch into two directions. Eventually, these branches can be followed backward all the way to a common African root—a common ancestor of us all.

DISCUSSION

Discuss these questions with a classmate.

1. How much of the article was a review of what you heard in the lecture?
2. What information in the reading surprised you?
3. Compare the concepts of natural selection, discussed in the reading, with selective breeding, discussed in the lecture. How are they similar and how do they differ? Do humans always make good choices when they breed animals and plants?

RESEARCH PROJECT

Individually or in a group, research one of the following topics. Write a short paper on the topic, or plan and present a group presentation to inform the class about the topic.

1. Research the mechanism of recessive inheritance and try to find examples of recessive traits that you share with your grandparents and not your parents.
2. Choose an area of the world that has a distinctive physical environment and research its plant and animal species. Analyze how the species have adapted to their environment.
3. Choose another related topic that interests you or your group.

CHAPTER 10

Genetic Engineering

Playing Roulette with Mother Nature's Designs?

TOPIC PREVIEW

Answer the following questions with a partner or your classmates.

1. Look at the title of this chapter. How do you think the term *playing roulette* relates to *genetic engineering*?
2. Discuss what you see in the photograph on this page. Why do you think this fish was developed?
3. What advantages and disadvantages does genetically engineered food present, in your opinion?

A biologist shows how genetic engineering enables growth in salmon.

BEFORE LISTENING

VOCABULARY PREVIEW

CD 4, TR 7

A **Read through the sentences below, which are missing vocabulary from the lecture. Listen to the sentences and write the missing words in the blanks.**

1. I'll be touching on some of the important advances that have been made in recent years using genetic engineering, and also some of the ________________ that have arisen.
2. The new DNA causes the ________________ to function in a different way, and this function or trait can then be inherited by ________________ generations.
3. One way to increase ________________ is to make plants ________________ to disease so that more of the crop survives and is harvested.
4. Transgenic Bt crops produce enough ________________ to actually kill the harmful insect, so farmers don't need to spray their crops with ________________.
5. If it is approved by the FDA—that's the U.S. government agency that ________________ food—the genetically modified salmon would be the first genetically altered animal to be approved for human ________________ in the United States.
6. The genetically altered fish has never been eaten before, and it could cause dangerous ________________, especially because seafood tends to be quite ________________.
7. ________________ are concerned that the fish will escape and breed with the wild salmon population, which is already ________________.
8. The FDA granted marketing approval for ________________ goat antithrombin, the first drug to be produced in genetically modified ________________.
9. ________________ have questions about gene therapy.
10. How long will it be before we're ________________—and maybe selecting—human ________________ for characteristics such as physical strength?

B **Check the spelling of the vocabulary words with your teacher. Discuss the meanings of these words and any other unfamiliar words in the sentences.**

PREDICTIONS

Think about the questions in the Topic Preview on page 99 and the sentences you heard in the Vocabulary Preview. Write three questions that you think will be answered in the lecture. Share your questions with your classmates.

NOTETAKING PREPARATION

Vocabulary: Recovering Meaning as You Listen

When an unfamiliar word or expression is used in a lecture, the lecturer will often follow it with a synonym or a definition, using a signal word or phrase. For example:

. . . , or . . .
. . . , that is, . . .
. . . ; in other words . . .

The synonym or definition will usually follow a pause and echo the stress and intonation of the word being defined. The lecturer is "replaying" the information by substituting the definition in place of the unfamiliar word or expression. Sometimes a lecturer will pause before a synonym or a definition, but not use a signal word. For example:

. . . the production of pharmaceuticals [pause] drugs [pause] *by genetic engineering . . .*

Be sure to pay attention to how an unfamiliar word is used in a sentence. You can usually learn enough of the meaning this way to follow the lecture.

Try not to spend time writing an unfamiliar word or expression. Just write the first letters and leave space with a question mark. Listen for a definition to put in the space. If you don't hear one, you can ask a classmate or the lecturer later.

A **Read the phrases on the left, which contain words that may be unfamiliar. Draw a line to match each phrase on the left with a phrase on the right that explains it.**

some controversies that have arisen, uh,	where the effect is on the body of only a particular individual
it develops a resistance to the toxin— in other words	specific concerns that some people have
This can be done in somatic cells, that is,	it takes more to kill it

CD 4, TR 8

B **Listen to the sentences from the lecture, which contain explanations of the words and expressions below. Take brief notes showing the meaning of each word.**

1. transgenic: ______________________
2. drought: ______________________
3. germ line cells: ______________________
4. cloning: ______________________
5. antithrombin: ______________________

FIRST LISTENING

CD 4, TR 9

Listen to the lecture and number the slides on this page and the next in the order they would be shown during the lecture. Write the number of the slide on the line provided and answer the question to the right of the slide.

Genetically Modified

Definition

Uses of genetic modification

In agriculture – GMOs
- examples
- main goal of GM

Slide #____

What percent of the cotton grown in the United States is genetically modified?

Genetic Engineering

Definition
- advances
- concerns

Slide #____

Name one of the fields in which genetic engineering has made great advances.

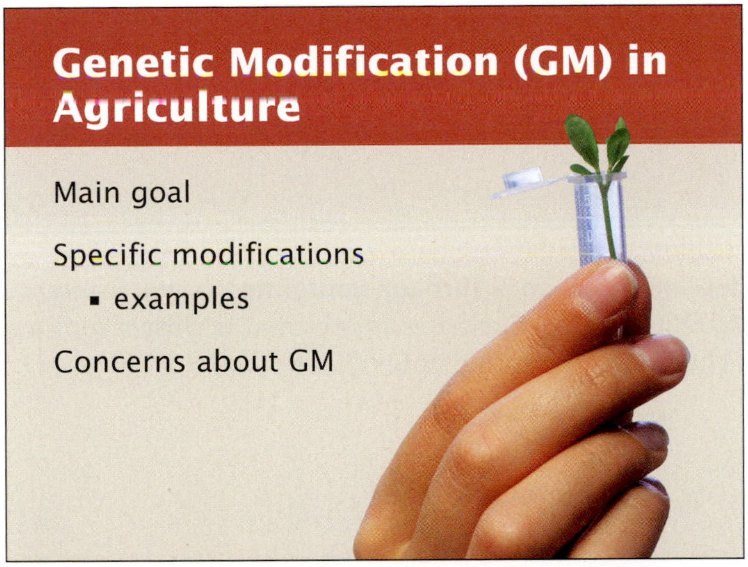

Slide #_____

What is the fastest growing area of agriculture today?

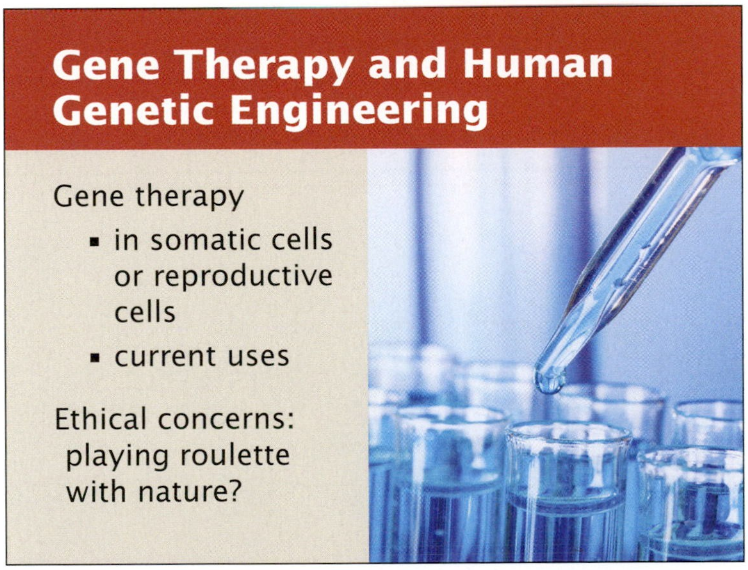

Slide #_____

How successful are the technology and use of gene therapy today?

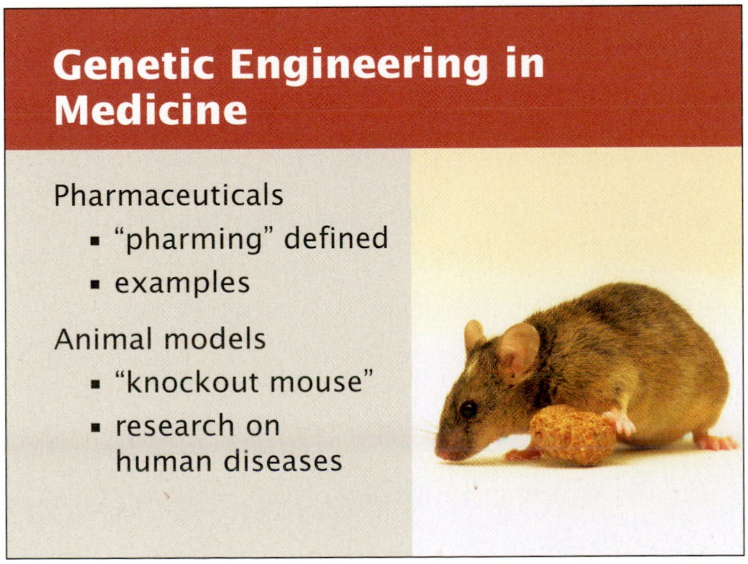

Slide #_____

Name two human diseases for which mouse models have been developed.

CD 4, TR 10

SECOND LISTENING

Now that you have listened to the lecture once, listen to it again and take notes. Write on a separate piece of paper.

CD 4, TR 11

THIRD LISTENING

You will hear parts of the lecture again. Look through your notes as you listen. A notetaking mentor will discuss the notes. Circle the answer that is closest to the notes you took, and put a check (✓) next to the notes that the mentor wrote.

Part 1

1. a.

Lect. prevu:
Genet engin'rng
- defn
- imprt. rcnt advcs (agr & med)
- ~~co~~ ppls' conc'ns ?
  pract & ethic'l

b.

Genet eng.
- what is?
- impor. advanc (rcnt)
- concns
  pract & ethicl

Projcts: agr & medcn

Part 2

2. a.

Why GMOs? ↗ fd prod – wrld pop ↗, agr land ↘
How ↗ prod?
GM → dz/insct resist
ex, Bt corn, potat, etc. Bt kills insct, dnt need spray. But PRBLM: Bt-resist – ex cotn India

b.

Considr why modf fds & how
- spcfc goals of GE in agr.
- how GMOs achv goals or try
- concerns

Prim goal: ↑ fd prod (area ag ↓, wrld pop ↑)
How? mk plnts dis & ins resist – ~~Basill~~ BT – toxin kills bad insects BUT org + toxin = resist to tox

Part 3

3. a.

farmasu ..? pharming – genet eng
= agric prod of ~~pharm...?~~ drugs
gn mks drug – drg in host plnt / anim – plnt / anml mks drg
If nd mr drg, clone tech to reprod
EX –safflower – mks ins
- transgen goat " antithro – prot – prevent bld clts

b.

GE drugs ("pharming")
1. usfl drug-prod gn
2. put " in anml/plnt
3. " prods drug

↘ $$ thn in lab
nd ↗ drg? Clone plnt/anml
EX: –saffl (oil) → insulin
–Xgen goat → antithrom_(?) – in mlk

AFTER LISTENING

ACCURACY CHECK

CD 4, TR 12

You will hear questions about the lecture. Answer each question by referring to the notes that you took while listening to the lecture.

1. a. protein from another plant or animal
   b. DNA from another plant or animal
   c. toxins from another plant or animal
2. a. engineering
   b. medicine
   c. agriculture
3. a. to produce more food
   b. to produce healthier livestock
   c. to produce improved crops
4. a. goats
   b. soybeans
   c. sheep
5. a. They kill harmful insects.
   b. They tend to be less healthy.
   c. Insects develop resistance to them.
6. a. It may cause allergies.
   b. It may be toxic.
   c. Both *a.* and *b.*
7. a. tendency to be overweight
   b. immune deficiency
   c. mental depression
8. a. screening embryos
   b. treating disease
   c. determining eye or hair color

ORAL SUMMARY

Use your notes to create an oral summary of the lecture with your partner. As you work together, add details to your notes that your partner included but you had missed.

DISCUSSION

Discuss the following questions with a classmate or in a small group.

1. Do you know whether genetically modified foods are sold in your country? How do you feel about eating GM food products?
2. The lecturer mentions that critics of transgenic salmon refer to it as "Frankenfish." Discuss what this reference means. Do you agree with the critics? Why or why not?
3. The lecturer asks, "Are we playing roulette with Mother Nature?" Discuss what this means and give your opinion.

PRE-READING

The following Reading is about transgenic crops and animals. Before you read, answer the following questions. Share your answers with a classmate.

1. Look at the title of the article and the photograph on the next page. Write two things that you expect to learn about transgenic crops from the article.
2. In the lecture, the speaker presented some advantages and disadvantages associated with genetically modified organisms. Which are you interested in learning about more: advantages or disadvantages? Explain.

READING

Now read the article.

Food: How Altered?

In the brave new world of genetic engineering, Dean DellaPenna envisions this cornucopia: tomatoes and broccoli bursting with cancer-fighting chemicals and vitamin-enhanced crops of rice, sweet potatoes, and cassava to help nourish the poor. He sees wheat, soy, and peanuts free of allergens; bananas that deliver vaccines; and vegetable oils so loaded with therapeutic ingredients that doctors "prescribe" them for patients at risk for cancer and heart disease. A plant biochemist at Michigan State University, DellaPenna believes that genetically engineered foods are the key to the next wave of advances in agriculture and health.

While DellaPenna and many others see great potential in the products of this new biotechnology, some see uncertainty, even danger. In North America and Europe, the value and impact of genetically engineered food crops have become subjects of intense debate, provoking reactions from unbridled optimism to fervent political opposition.

Just what are genetically engineered foods, and who is eating them? What do we know about their benefits—and their risks? What effect might engineered plants have on the environment and on agricultural practices around the world? Can they help solve the problem of feeding and preserving the health of the Earth's burgeoning population?

Most people in the United States don't realize that they've been eating genetically engineered foods since the mid-1990s. And in fact, genetic modification is much older than that. Humans have been altering the genetic makeup of plants for millennia, keeping seeds from the best crops and planting them in following years, breeding and crossbreeding varieties to make them taste sweeter, grow bigger, last longer. But the technique of genetic engineering is new and quite different from conventional breeding. Traditional breeders cross-related organisms whose genetic makeups are similar. In so doing, they transfer tens of thousands of genes. By contrast, today's genetic engineers can transfer just a few genes at a time between species that are distantly related or not related at all.

The engineered organisms produced by transferring genes between species are referred to as "transgenic." Several dozen transgenic food crops are currently on the market, among them varieties of corn, squash, canola, soybeans, and cotton, from which cottonseed oil is produced. Most of these crops are engineered to help farmers deal with age-old agriculture problems: weeds, insects, and disease.

With the new tools of genetic engineering, scientists have also created transgenic animals. Atlantic salmon grow more slowly during the winter, but

Researcher monitoring modified plant cell growth in specimen dishes

engineered salmon, "improved" by the insertion of modified growth-hormone genes from other fish, reach market size in about half the normal time [see the photo on page 99]. These transgenic salmon have not yet entered the market.

Whether biotech foods will deliver on their promise of eliminating world hunger and bettering the lives of all remains to be seen. Their potential is enormous, yet they carry risks—and we may pay for accidents or errors in judgment in ways we cannot yet imagine. But the biggest mistake of all would be to blindly reject or endorse this new technology. If we analyze carefully how, where, and why we introduce genetically altered products, and if we test them thoroughly and judge them wisely, we can weigh their risks against their benefits to those who need them most.

DISCUSSION

Discuss these questions with a classmate.

1. What is Dean DellaPenna's attitude about genetically modified organisms (GMOs)? How does his attitude compare with that of the lecturer?
2. How would you compare the attitudes of the author and the lecturer toward GMOs? Support your opinion.
3. What did you learn from the article that you didn't hear in the lecture?

RESEARCH PROJECT

Individually or in a group, research one of the following topics. Write a short paper on the topic, or plan and present a group presentation to inform the class about the topic.

1. Labeling of GM food products: What laws exist in the United States? In other countries?
2. Animal models of human diseases: What diseases are being researched today? Is progress being made?
3. Genetically modified salmon: At the time this lecture was given, the U.S. FDA had not yet approved the sale of GM salmon. Has that changed? Is GM salmon still controversial?
4. Gene therapy: What recent advances (if any) have been made? What risks are currently associated with gene therapy?
5. Choose another related topic that interests you or your group.

UNIT 5 VIDEO

The Human Journey

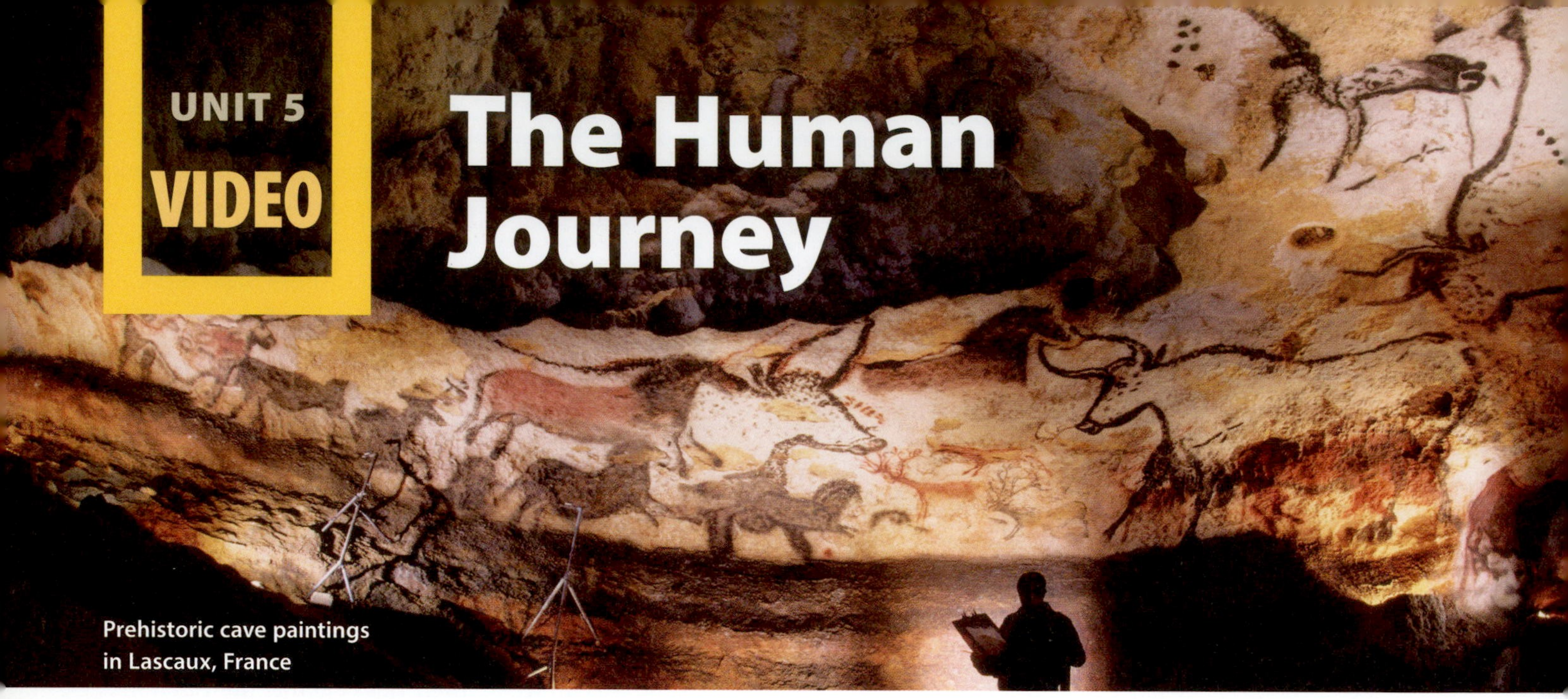

Prehistoric cave paintings in Lascaux, France

BEFORE VIEWING

TOPIC PREVIEW

Fill in your family tree below. Then talk with a partner about what physical traits, such as eye color or height, and personality traits, such as shyness or friendliness, you have inherited from different members of your family.

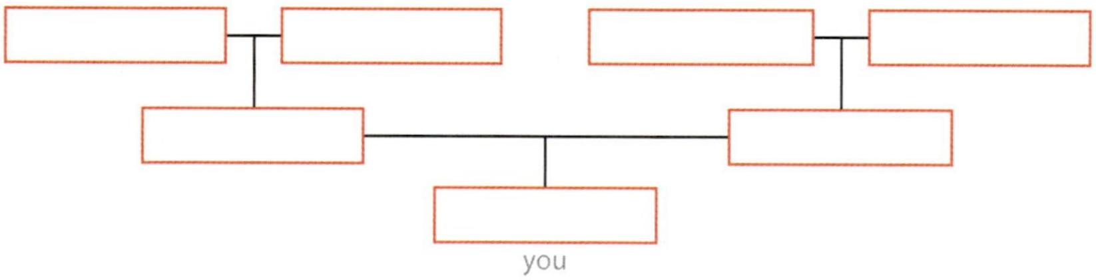

VOCABULARY PREVIEW

A **Read the definitions of these key words and phrases that you will hear during the video.**

spring from come from
paleoanthropology the study of ancient humans, primarily through fossils
direct lines of descent series of people born in a family going back through time from parent to child
ancestry relationships to people going back many generations into the past
genealogy the study of family history and relationships back through many generations
trace back follow back in time or place
pass it on to their children give their children the same DNA or genes as they have
lineages members of one's family going back through history from parent to child
maternal relating to a mother
paternal relating to a father

B **Work with a partner and discuss answers to the following questions.**

1. Are you interested in **genealogy**? How far can you **trace back** your family?
2. What is something that you would like to **pass on to your children**?
3. What sorts of things do you think a **paleoanthropologist** can discover?
4. Who in your culture comes from a famous **lineage**, in other words, they can trace their **line of descent** back to someone famous?
5. Do you have any famous **ancestry**?
6. Have you ever heard the idea that humans **spring from** aliens who visited this planet millions of years ago? What do you think of this idea?
7. What do you know about your **paternal** and **maternal** grandparents?

VIEWING

FIRST VIEWING

Watch the video, and then compare your first impressions with a partner. Talk about what you remember, what surprised you, and what interested you.

SECOND VIEWING

Watch the video again. Listen for the missing words and write them in the blanks.

1. Well, historically, these questions have been approached through the study of stones and ____________________.
2. In our DNA, inside of nearly every cell in our body, DNA that we've ____________________ from those parents, grandparents, great-grandparents and so on, and this traces an unbroken line of descent going back in ____________________.
3. So if you have mitochondrial DNA, which everyone in the room does, you got it from your ____________________, and she got it from her ____________________.
4. By looking at the pattern of these genetic variants, these random ____________________ that have occurred over time, on both of these lineages, we can construct family ____________________ for everybody alive today.

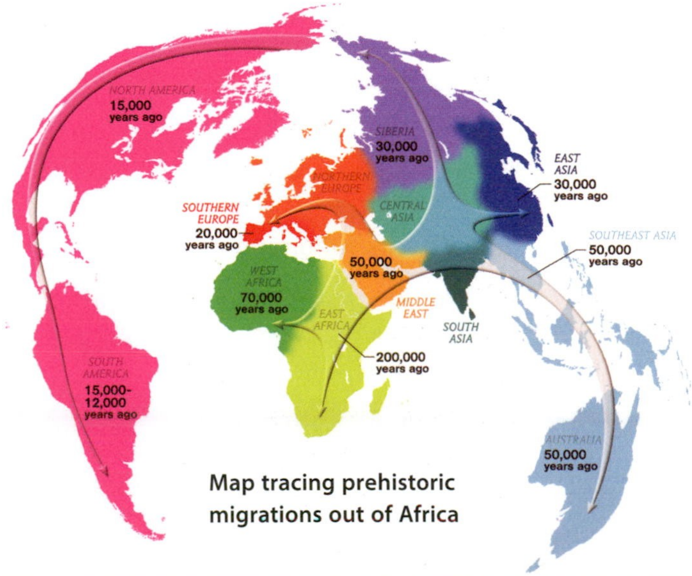

Map tracing prehistoric migrations out of Africa

THIRD VIEWING

Complete these notes as you watch the video. Use abbreviations and symbols.

RQs = How expl patterns of ______________________________?
= Are we all ______________________________?
= Why occ all ______________________________?

1) Poss answ
   a) study of ______________________________
      - but only leads to poss ≠ probs.
   b) genetics → ______________________________

2) Genetics vs geneology
   a) gen'logy → brick wall
   b) DNA can trace ______________________________

3) We can study
   a) mitochondrial DNA ______________________________
   b) Y-chromosome from ______________________________
   c) genetic variants

   → ______________________________

AFTER VIEWING

ORAL SUMMARY

Use your notes to create an oral summary of the video with your partner. As you work together, add details to your notes that your partner included but you had missed.

DISCUSSION

Discuss the following questions with a classmate or in a small group.

1. How does studying history through paleoanthropology and archaeology differ from Spencer Wells' approach as a geneticist?
2. Spencer Wells says "it turns out there is a written document in effect, that we're all carrying around inside of ourselves." What does he mean by this?
3. What do you know about how scientists' understanding of DNA has influenced the fields of agriculture, medicine, and crime fighting?

Audioscripts

UNIT 1

Anthropology: The Study of Humans and Their Creations

CHAPTER 1

Anthropologists: Working in a Diverse Profession

VOCABULARY PREVIEW Page 3

A

1. As Paul Bohannan, renowned anthropologist, pointed out a number of years ago, "Each science that deals with people has its own definitions of *human*."
2. Anthropology attempts to be inclusive—the study of human behavior in all places and throughout time.
3. Mostly the work of anthropologists is not glamorous and involves repetitive and tedious activities.
4. In the modern day, anthropology is a recognized social science with two broad fields and several branches or subfields.
5. Archaeology is the study of different cultures through material sources rather than direct interviews or observations of the group under study.
6. Linguistics, as you probably know, is the study of language as communication among humans.
7. Culture is learned and transmitted primarily through language.
8. Ethnography is the systematic description of human societies, mostly based on firsthand fieldwork.
9. It is important to note that there are several universals common among all societies.
10. So, you might ask, what are the practical applications for such a broad field?

NOTETAKING PREPARATION Page 4

B

1. The two broad fields are physical anthropology and cultural anthropology.
2. Physical anthropology is concerned with the development of man as a mammal.
3. Related subjects are anatomy, biology, and paleontology.
4. Physical anthropologists study the evolution of the human species.
5. One way they do this is by the comparative analysis of fossils.

FIRST LISTENING Page 5

Lecturer: The Greek word for "man" is *anthropos* and the word *anthropology* has been in the English language for centuries. But just what does the word mean? Literally, *anthropology* means "the study of man." However, as British philosopher Alfred North Whitehead noted, "It is a well-founded, historical generalization that the last thing to be discovered in any science is what the science is really about." And as Paul Bohannan, renowned anthropologist, pointed out a number of years ago, "Each science that deals with people has its own definitions of *human*. An economist," he explains, "defines a human as a choice-making animal. Philosophers define man as a rationalizing animal." Anthropology attempts to be inclusive—the study of human behavior in all places and throughout time. It specializes in the description of humanistic, scientific, biological, historical, psychological, and social views of humans.

To paraphrase Barbara Miller's statement in her textbook *Cultural Anthropology*, the popular impression of anthropology is based mainly on movies and television shows that depict anthropologists as adventurers and heroes. Some do have adventures and discover treasures in Egyptian tombs and elsewhere, but mostly, their work is less glamorous and involves repetitive and tedious activities. Until around the middle of the nineteenth century, *anthropology* was a term used for all of the humanities subjects. My lecture today explains the fields and branches of anthropology. We're going to begin by stating that anthropology is the study of human behavior in all places and at all times.

Western civilization takes credit for the development of anthropology, which, as a matter of fact, was a relatively late science. Earlier Greek and Roman philosophers were more interested in speculating about the ideal society rather than describing those known to them.

After the onset of the Age of Exploration, which included the discovery of the Americas, as well as travel to other distant places, the study of non–Western people began in earnest. In the modern day, anthropology is a recognized social science with two broad fields and several branches or subfields.

The two broad fields are physical anthropology and cultural anthropology. Let me give you a brief description of each. Physical anthropology is concerned with the development of man as a mammal. Related subjects are anatomy, biology, and paleontology. Physical anthropologists study the evolution of the human species. One way they do this is by the comparative analysis of fossils—preserved remnants of once-living creatures and living primates, which include human beings or Homo sapiens. Common fossils are shells, bones, and molds or imprints. These are found buried in the earth or permanently frozen in glaciers. Living primates are analyzed in order to study the mechanics of evolution and genetic differences among human populations.

Next let's talk about cultural anthropology. This field is the study of learned behavior in human societies. Most cultural anthropologists limit themselves to a few geographic areas, for example, Margaret Mead in Samoa and New Guinea, and Clyde Kluckhohn with the Navajo Indians in the Southwestern United States. And, I should mention that Kluckhohn's work *Mirror for Man* is considered one of the best introductions to anthropology. Cultural anthropology and the scientific study of human culture will be discussed in more detail in our next lecture. The subfields of cultural anthropology are archaeology, linguistics, and ethnography.

Now, archaeology is the study of different cultures through material sources rather than direct interviews or observations of the group under study. One example of a famous archaeological site discovered in the last century was King Tut's tomb near Luxor, Egypt, in 1922.

So, linguistics, as you probably know, is the study of language as communication among humans. Culture is learned and transmitted primarily through language.

Ethnography is the systematic description of human societies, mostly based on firsthand fieldwork. Based on ethnographies, anthropologists provide ethnologies or explanations of the behavior of different peoples. Another subfield of ethnography is social anthropology. Social anthropology is concerned with people as social beings. A related subject is, of course, sociology.

Let me also mention briefly psychological anthropology, which deals with human personality and feelings. These are greatly influenced by an individual's biological and mental characteristics, as well as physical surroundings and personal experiences. Related subjects are psychology and psychiatry.

It is important to note that there are several universals common among all societies; for example, the basic similarities in human biology and the existence of two sexes. Another of these is education—either formal or informal, or both. Education is necessary to provide the young with the skills and attitudes needed to carry on as adults.

So, you might ask, what are the practical applications for such a broad field? The answer is that anthropology helps us plan the future and helps us contribute to the solution of human problems. This newest area of the study of man is applied anthropology. Formerly, anthropology was limited to the academic field. Anthropologists were teachers or museum curators. But for the past several decades, large numbers of "anthro" graduates have been employed in fields such as urban planning and administration, health care, and international development. Most important is that although anthropologists have taken up the task of documenting the processes and changes of cultures past and present, they also provide the necessary insights into where the human species is heading.

SECOND LISTENING Page 7

See First Listening, above.

THIRD LISTENING Page 7

Part 1

Lecturer: Next let's talk about cultural anthropology. This field is the study of learned behavior in human societies. Most cultural anthropologists limit themselves to a few geographic areas, for example, Margaret Mead in Samoa and New Guinea, and Clyde Kluckhohn with the Navajo Indians in the Southwestern United States. And, I should mention that Kluckhohn's work *Mirror for Man* is considered one of the best introductions to anthropology.

Mentor

1. *Look at number one. Which notes are similar to your notes? Did you use abbreviations?*

   Notes a *are my notes. If you circled* b, *you are taking too much time because you are writing complete words. Use abbreviations.*

2. *Now look at number two. Which notes are similar to your notes? Did you hear the second name? Kluckhohn? Did you know how to spell it?*

   The notes in a *are not good because it looks like Margaret Mead worked in the Southwestern United States.*

   The notes in b *and* c *are good. I wrote the notes in* b. *I didn't know the spelling of* Kluckhohn, *but I could later ask a classmate or the professor for the spelling.*

Part 2

Lecturer: Cultural anthropology and the scientific study of human culture will be discussed in more detail in our next lecture. The subfields of cultural anthropology are archaeology, linguistics, and ethnography.

Mentor

3. *Look at number three. Which notes are similar to your notes?*

   Notes b *contain information that is not important. Notes* a *do not show that the last three items, archaeology, linguistics, and ethnography, are subfields of cultural anthropology. These notes do not show the relationship of the ideas.*

   The notes in c *are mine.*

Part 3

Lecturer: Archaeology is the study of different cultures through material sources rather than direct interviews or observations of the group under study. One example of a famous archaeological site discovered in the last century was King Tut's tomb near Luxor, Egypt, in 1922.

Mentor

4. *Look at number four. Which notes are similar to your notes?*

   Notes a *are difficult to read. Does* d-i-f-f *mean* difficult *or* different*? Does* i-n-t *mean intense, interest, or something else? The abbreviations are too short.*

   Notes b *are mine. I used abbreviations that were a bit longer than the notes in* a. *I will be able to read these notes later and understand them. I also underlined the important words* material sources.

   Notes c *are easy to read, but they are too long. Do not write every verb, article, and preposition. Abbreviate as much as possible and only write important words in your notes, not complete sentences.*

ACCURACY CHECK Page 8

1. What is the literal definition of *anthropology*?
2. What were early Greeks and Romans interested in?
3. Which discovery took place in the Age of Exploration?
4. Which area of study listed is *not* a major area of study in anthropology?
5. What is anthropologist Margaret Mead well-known for?
6. What is the word for an explanation of the behavior of different peoples?
7. The lecturer mentioned education. What is education an example of?
8. What is an example of an area of work for someone interested in applied anthropology?

CHAPTER 2

The Concept of Culture: Understanding One Another

VOCABULARY PREVIEW Page 12

A

1. Culture is that complex whole which includes knowledge, belief, art, law, morals, custom, and any other capabilities and habits acquired by man as a member of society.
2. Another definition of culture that many find useful is, "the totality of learned, socially transmitted behavior."
3. Ned Seelye, in his 1993 book *Teaching Culture*, lists six skills to nurture and support intercultural communication.
4. Cultivate curiosity about another culture and empathy toward its members.
5. Recognize that different roles and other social variables such as age, sex, social class, religion, ethnicity, and place of residence affect the way people speak and behave.
6. Realize that effective communication requires discovering the culturally conditioned images of people when they think, act, and react to the world around them.
7. Recognize that situational variables and conventions shape people's behavior in important ways.
8. Understand that people generally act the way they do because they are exercising the options their society allows for satisfying basic physical and psychological needs.
9. Culture and society must coexist.
10. In the long history of human life, multiculturalism is a fairly recent phenomenon.

NOTETAKING PREPARATION Page 13

B

Lecturer: Why study cultural anthropology? One reason noted by Ruth Benedict, another well-known anthropologist, is that the story of humanity from the Stone Age to the present is such a fascinating one of cultural growth. Interestingly, according to Tylor's and Morgan's cultural development theories, every society has gone through three stages or steps. These are savagery, barbarism, and finally, civilization. The last is, of course, to varying degrees.

We are often reminded of another compelling reason to learn about different cultures—to learn and use a foreign language effectively. Most of us realize that just knowing the language of another culture is not enough for meaningful communication. You can ask anyone who has tried to use their high school Spanish inside a Spanish-speaking country.

FIRST LISTENING Page 14

Lecturer: Let me begin the lecture today by asking, "What exactly is culture?" This question has been approached by anthropologists in many different ways. Murdock, for example, in *Outline of World Cultures*, produced what many have called the ultimate laundry list of things cultural by naming 900-odd categories of human behavior. I won't attempt to go into these at this time. Another less lengthy list is the famous "grocery list" of Edward B. Tylor. He wrote, "Culture is that complex whole which includes knowledge, belief, art, law, morals, custom, and any other capabilities and habits acquired by man as a member of society." But another definition of culture that many find useful is Kessing's, "the totality of learned, socially transmitted behavior." Obviously this definition leaves out much if we feel obligated to include all the ways of life that have been evolved by people in every society.

A particular culture, then, would mean the total shared way of life of a given group. This would include their ways of thinking, acting, and feeling as reflected in their religion, law, language, art, and customs, as well as concrete things such as houses, clothing, and tools.

Cultural anthropology is the study of cultures—living and dead. In its totality, it includes linguistics, the study of speech forms; archaeology, the study of dead cultures; and ethnology, which is the study of living cultures or those that can be observed directly.

So, why study cultural anthropology? One reason noted by Ruth Benedict, another well-known anthropologist, is that the story of humanity from the Stone Age to the present is such a fascinating one of cultural growth. Interestingly, according to Tylor's and Morgan's cultural development theories, every society has gone through three stages or steps. These are savagery, barbarism, and finally, civilization. The last is, of course, to varying degrees.

We are often reminded of another compelling reason to learn about different cultures—to learn and use a foreign language effectively. Most of us realize that just knowing the language of another culture is not enough for meaningful communication. You can ask anyone who has tried to use their high school Spanish inside a Spanish-speaking country.

Ned Seelye, in his 1993 book *Teaching Culture*, lists six skills to nurture and support intercultural communication:

Number 1: Cultivate curiosity about another culture and empathy toward its members.

Number 2: Recognize that different roles and other social variables such as age, sex, social class, religion, ethnicity, and place of residence affect the way people speak and behave.

Number 3: Realize that effective communication requires discovering the culturally conditioned images of people when they think, act, and react to the world around them.

Number 4: Recognize that situational variables and conventions shape people's behavior in important ways.

Number 5: Understand that people generally act the way they do because they are exercising the options their society allows for satisfying basic physical and psychological needs.

And, finally, number 6: Develop the ability to evaluate the truth of a generalization about the target culture and to locate and organize information about the target culture from books, mass media, people, and personal observations.

Culture and society must coexist. Without living together, people cannot create a culture or a way of life. If a group or society is small, isolated, and stable, it might also share a single culture. In fact, there are still what are called "uncontacted peoples," groups of people who live in very remote areas of the rain forest in Peru and Brazil who probably share a single culture. And now, instead of making contact in order to study them, cultural anthropologists and governments of these countries are making efforts to protect their regions from intrusions.

It is important to remember, however, that large societies, such as those in Canada, the United States, India, or Egypt, are multicultural or "pluralist" societies. They also tend to have many subcultures. In the long history of human life, multiculturalism is a fairly recent phenomenon. Those of us in multicultural environments must remember that discovering similarities among people from different cultures is as important as identifying differences. For example, in classrooms on just about every university campus in the world, we find students from many different social and ethnic backgrounds. What are some of the "universals" that you and other international students have all experienced in your earlier educational life?

One common universal is that all cultures use rewards and punishments to encourage correct behavior. Another example is that societies withhold certain information from the young. This might include faults in our leaders or sexual taboos. A third universal is the effort by the controlling group in a culture to educate the young to strengthen and secure its dominant position. In the majority of contemporary societies this control is reached through political means in contrast to the military actions of earlier times, such as the Roman Conquests and the Moorish invasions.

In closing this lecture on societies and culture, let me remind you not to forget the contributions of thoughts and actions of the individual person in a group. Note the observation of Edward Sapir, another famous anthropologist: "It is always the individual that really thinks and acts and dreams and revolts." Obviously the concept of culture will be argued by anthropologists for years to come.

SECOND LISTENING Page 16

See First Listening, above.

THIRD LISTENING Page 16

Part 1

Lecturer: Cultural anthropology is the study of cultures—living and dead. In its totality, it includes linguistics, the study of speech forms; archaeology, the study of dead cultures; and ethnology, which is the study of living cultures or those that can be observed directly.

Mentor

1. *Look at number one. Which is similar to your notes—*a *or* b*? Did you make a list?*

   I wrote notes b. *The list in* b *is much easier to read. The notes in* b *will be easier to use later to study from.*

Part 2

Lecturer: Ned Seelye, in his 1993 book *Teaching Culture*, lists six skills to nurture and support intercultural communication:

Number 1: Cultivate curiosity about another culture and empathy toward its members.

Number 2: Recognize that different roles and other social variables such as age, sex, social class, religion, ethnicity, and place of residence affect the way people speak and behave.

Number 3: Realize that effective communication requires discovering the culturally conditioned images of people when they think, act, and react to the world around them.

Number 4: Recognize that situational variables and conventions shape people's behavior in important ways.

Number 5: Understand that people generally act the way they do because they are exercising the options their society allows for satisfying basic physical and psychological needs.

And, finally, number 6: Develop the ability to evaluate the truth of a generalization about the target culture and to locate and organize information about the target culture from books, mass media, people, and personal observations.

Mentor

2. *Look at number two. In this part, the lecturer clearly introduced a list and said how many items would be in it. The lecturer said, "Ned Seelye, in his 1993 book* Teaching Culture, *lists six skills to nurture and support intercultural communication."*

   Was the beginning of your list similar to a, b, *or* c*? Both* a *and* b *have headings above the list. Headings are very important. If your notes are like* c, *your notes will not be very helpful because you won't know the significance of the items in the list.*

   The heading in a *is misleading. The skills are not related to teaching culture. They are skills related to communicating with different cultures.*

   My notes are b. *I didn't know how to spell* Seelye *and will have to find out in the book or by asking the professor.*

Part 3

Lecturer: What are some of the "universals" that you and other international students have all experienced in your earlier educational life?

One common universal is that all cultures use rewards and punishments to encourage correct behavior. Another example is that societies withhold certain information from the young. This might include faults in our leaders or sexual taboos. A third universal is the effort by the controlling group in a culture to educate the young to strengthen and secure its dominant position. In the majority of contemporary societies this control is reached through political means in contrast to the military actions of earlier times, such as the Roman conquests and the Moorish invasions.

Mentor

3. *Look at number three. Which notes are most similar to your notes for this part of the lecture?*

   The notes in a *and* c *clearly show the list of universals. These lists will be easy to read later. I made the notes in* c. *I included the reasons for the universals, to encourage correct behavior, for example.*

   If your notes are similar to a, *you might not have all the information you need for a test on this lecture.*

   If your notes are similar to b, *perhaps you didn't hear the lecturer signal that a list was coming. The lecturer asked a question—"What are some of the universals?"—then answered the question with "one common universal is." The use of the word* one *signaled that there would be more than one.*

ACCURACY CHECK Page 17

1. Who wrote a book called *Outline of World Cultures*?
2. Which is *not* one of Tylor's and Morgan's three stages of cultural growth?
3. When did Ned Seelye write his book *Teaching Culture*?
4. What is Seelye's first skill related to?
5. What is an example of a group that might share a single culture?

6. What is a recent phenomenon in the long history of human life?
7. By what means do most dominant cultural groups stay in control nowadays?
8. "It is always the individual that really thinks and acts and dreams and revolts." Who made that observation?

UNIT 2

History: The Passing of Time and Civilizations

CHAPTER 3

The Egyptian Pyramids: Houses of Eternity

VOCABULARY PREVIEW Page 25

A

1. To many people throughout the world, some of the most remarkable and puzzling monuments of ancient times are the pyramids of ancient Egypt.
2. Even though many of the pyramids are in ruins, they still give us some idea of the magnificence of ancient Egypt's civilization.
3. Remember, when we're talking about ancient Egypt, we're talking about at least 30 consecutive dynasties.
4. So when a person died, and especially when a pharaoh died, in order to ensure his eternal life, he had his body embalmed or mummified.
5. In other words, he had his corpse dried out and wrapped in linen to preserve it from decay.
6. You see, the ancient Egyptians really believed that if one's mummy was destroyed, then his or her soul would be destroyed
7. For another thing, the ancient Egyptians believed that the dead person could take his or her earthly possessions along to the next world.
8. Anyway, the dead person was provided with food, clothing, furniture, weapons, and even servants.
9. It seems that local builders and conquerors found it convenient to strip off the limestone from the pyramids and use it to build with.
10. And yet, what is so ironic is that even these tombs did not escape the attacks of the grave robbers.

NOTETAKING PREPARATION Page 26

B

Lecturer

1. The Fourth Dynasty covered the period from 2614 to 2502 BCE.
2. It has been estimated that 2.3 million blocks of limestone were used to build the Great Pyramid.
3. The blocks averaged 2,500 kilograms each.
4. The largest stone block weighs about 15,000 kilos.
5. In terms of height, the pyramid was originally 147 meters high, but today the top 10 meters are missing.
6. Khafre's pyramid was originally 3 meters lower than the Great Pyramid; however, today it is only 0.8 meters lower.

FIRST LISTENING Page 27

Lecturer: To many people throughout the world, some of the most remarkable and puzzling monuments of ancient times are the pyramids of ancient Egypt. You know, almost nothing at all remains of the great cities of the rulers of Egypt, the pharaohs. Time and weather have been really hard on ancient Egypt's cities and towns, but several of the temples, statues, and, most important of all, the pyramids have survived. Even though many of the pyramids are in ruins, they still give us some idea of the magnificence of ancient Egypt's civilization—a civilization that, um, after all, lasted for more than 3,000 years. Remember, when we're talking about ancient Egypt, we're talking about at least 30 consecutive dynasties. A dynasty is a series of kings or queens of the same royal family—something like the Romanovs of Russia, the Ming dynasty of China, or the Al Saud of Saudi Arabia.

As many of you probably already know, the pyramids were constructed as tombs, or burial places, for the Egyptian pharaohs and their family members. You see, the ancient Egyptians passionately believed in life after death. In fact, their entire culture revolved around that belief. The kings, queens, and state officials often spent an entire lifetime preparing for their life after death. They did this by collecting possessions, or "grave goods," by building tombs, and so forth. The Egyptians believed that they could be assured of an afterlife only if their bodies could be preserved from decay or destruction. So when a person died, and especially when a pharaoh died, in order to ensure eternal life, the person's body was embalmed, or mummified. In other words, the corpse was dried out and wrapped in linen to preserve it from decay. Then this "mummy" was hidden. This whole idea may seem quite strange today, but the ancient Egyptians really believed that if one's mummy was destroyed, then his or her soul would be destroyed, and if, on the other hand, the mummy—the dead body—was preserved, the soul would be immortal. Let me repeat that. If one's mummy was preserved, the soul would go on living.

For another thing, the ancient Egyptians believed that the dead person could take his or her earthly possessions along to the next world—this is just the opposite of the Western idea that "you can't take it with you when you go." Anyway, the dead person was provided with food, clothing, furniture, weapons, and even servants. It was not at all unusual for the pharaoh's slaves to be put to death so that they could serve him in his afterlife.

So you can see why the pharaohs wanted to have their bodies and their possessions hidden to protect them from grave robbers. Before they died, they had special tombs built for this purpose—to hide their bodies and their treasures. In the early years of ancient Egypt, these tombs were the pyramids—vast burial chambers that were built to fool the grave robbers. Unfortunately, the grave robbers almost always outsmarted even the most powerful and the most careful of pharaohs. They broke into most of the pyramids, that is the tombs, and stole the food and treasures they found. They even desecrated and destroyed the mummies of the dead. Needless to say, they would not bother a poor person's grave. These grave robbers even banded together into organizations, or brotherhoods. Just imagine, a grave robbers' union!

Now, as for the actual construction of the pyramids, it was during the First and Second Dynasties that the pharaohs and nobles of Egypt began to construct the type of tomb called the "mastaba." The First and Second Dynasties lasted from about 3100 until 2665 BCE. *Mastaba*, by the way, comes from an Arabic word meaning "bench" or "long seat." A mastaba looked like a low, flat-topped rectangle—something like a low bench or a shoebox. Essentially, the pointed pyramid was no more than an extension upward of the flat-topped mastaba.

The first "typical" pyramid—or at least what most people generally think a pyramid looks like—was built during the Third Dynasty, which lasted roughly from about 2664 until 2615 BCE. This pyramid was built for King Zoser—that's spelled *Z-o-s-e-r*—in about 2650 BCE. It was built by an architect named Imhotep—*I-m-h-o-t-e-p*. This pyramid was constructed as a series of giant steps. It, along with others of its type, is called a step pyramid. It was really simply a pile of mastabas, each step smaller and higher than the one before.

Actually, it was not until the Fourth Dynasty that the most famous pyramids were built. The three pyramids of Giza belong to the Fourth Dynasty—the Fourth Dynasty covered the period from 2614 to 2502 BCE. The three pyramids are located near the town of Giza, on the west bank of the Nile River, just outside the capital city of Egypt—Cairo. These three pyramids are really the very best preserved of all the Egyptian pyramids. The largest of the three is known as the Great Pyramid. And great it is! It was built for King Khufu—that's *K-h-u-f-u*. Khufu was called Cheops—*C-h-e-o-p-s*—by the Greeks, and so the pyramid is sometimes called the Pyramid of Cheops.

It has been estimated that 2.3 million blocks of limestone were used to build the Great Pyramid. The blocks averaged 2,500 kilograms each. The largest stone block weighs about 15,000 kilos. The base of the pyramid covers 5.3 hectares—an area large enough to hold 10 football fields. There's a story that the conqueror Napoleon once sat in the shadow of the Great Pyramid and calculated that the mass of stone in the pyramid could be used to build a wall 3 meters high by 0.3 meters thick around the entire country of France. In terms of height, the pyramid was originally 147 meters high, but today the top 10 meters are missing, and the entire outer limestone covering has been stripped away. It seems that local builders and conquerors found it convenient to strip off the limestone from the pyramids and use it to build with.

The Great Pyramid of Khufu is considered a wonder of ancient architecture. When you look at it, you immediately wonder how on earth the ancient Egyptians ever managed to build such a structure with no modern machinery such as cranes, bulldozers, and so forth, and with no iron tools. They had to cut the big limestone blocks with tools made of copper, which is a rather soft metal. But they managed to do it. The ancient Greek historian, Herodotus—that's *H-e-r-o-d-o-t-u-s*—Herodotus said that 400,000 men worked for 20 years to build the Great Pyramid.

Archaeologists today doubt these figures, but, of course, the true statistics cannot ever really be determined. It is thought, though, that at least 100,000 people worked to build any single pyramid. Most of these workers were slaves. They worked on the tombs during times when the Nile River overflowed its banks and covered the fields. The Nile's flooding made farming impossible and made transportation of the stone to the pyramid site easier.

The second and third pyramids at Giza were built by Khufu's successors. The tomb of Khafre is the second pyramid at Giza—Khafre is spelled *K-h-a-f-r-e*. Khafre's pyramid was originally 3 meters lower than the Great Pyramid; however, today it is only 0.8 meters lower. Its present height is 136.2 meters. The third pyramid, built for Menkaure, covers only half the area occupied by the Great Pyramid and is only 62.5 meters high. Menkaure is spelled *M-e-n-k-a-u-r-e*.

None of the later pyramids that were built during the next 13 or 14 centuries were nearly as large or as magnificent as the pyramids at Giza. And even though pyramid building continued right up into the Eleventh and Twelfth Dynasties—that was up through about 1786 BCE—it was becoming increasingly clear to the pharaohs and the nobles of Egypt that the pyramid method of burial provided very little or no protection at all for their mummies and possessions. The pyramids were, of course, impressive and lasting monuments, but they were all too visible. They invited grave robbers to try to break into them. And so eventually, one of the pharaohs, King Thutmose I, decided to sacrifice publicity for safety in the construction of his House of Eternity. I don't need to spell Thutmose for you, do I?

Instead of ordering the construction of a pyramid, Thutmose had his tomb dug out of the rock of a valley far from the Nile River and far from Cairo. The spot he chose was some 11 kilometers from the river on its west bank. The area is now known as the Valley of the Kings. Many pharaohs followed Thutmose's example. After him, most of the pharaohs abandoned aboveground pyramid construction in favor of underground hiding places as the burial places for their precious royal bones. And yet, what is so ironic is that even these tombs did not escape the grave robbers, persistent devils that they were!

I'll end this discussion by pointing out that, when the ancient Greeks first saw the Great Pyramids of Egypt, the pyramids were already 2,000 years old. The Greeks called them one of the Seven Wonders of the World. Almost nothing remains of the other six Wonders—the Hanging Gardens of Babylon, the Temple of Diana, and so on—but the three mighty pyramids of Giza, as well as 32 other recognizable pyramids, still stand. These pyramids of Egypt are monuments to a great and ancient civilization and to people's endless search for eternal recognition and eternal life.

SECOND LISTENING Page 29

See First Listening, above.

THIRD LISTENING Page 29

Part 1

Lecturer: Time and weather have been really hard on ancient Egypt's cities and towns, but several of the temples, statues, and, most important of all, the pyramids have survived. Even though many of the pyramids are in ruins, they still give us some idea of the magnificence of ancient Egypt's civilization—a civilization that, um, after all, lasted for more than 3,000 years. Remember, when we're talking about ancient Egypt, we're talking about at least 30 consecutive dynasties. A dynasty is a series of kings or queens of the same royal family—something like the Romanovs of Russia, the Ming dynasty of China, or the Al Saud of Saudi Arabia.

Mentor

1. *Look at number one. What did you put in your notes for the word* Egypt*? Did you use an abbreviation? Use abbreviations that you will be able to figure out later when you look at your notes. My abbreviation is* b.
2. *Now look at number two. Did you use an abbreviation for the word* pyramids*? My abbreviation is* b.

   Both Egypt *and* pyramids *are used very frequently in the lecture. If you circled* a, *for questions 1 and 2, you are writing too much.*
3. *Look at number three. Circle the note that looks most like your notes. If you wrote* d, *you wrote too much. My note is* c. *I used the abbreviation* y-r-s *for the word* years *and the number* 3 *and abbreviation* K *for three thousand. If you did you that, you are taking very accurate and efficient notes.*
4. *Now look at number four. Do your notes look more like* a *or* b*? I wrote* a. *It is a definition of dynasty. It's a good idea to write a definition if you didn't already know it or if the lecturer is defining something in a new way. Note* b *lists the other dynasties. If you listed those, you really shouldn't have. This example might help you to understand the definition, but it wasn't important information about the topic of the lecture. Write the important information, not extraneous details.*

Part 2

Lecturer: Now, as for the actual construction of the pyramids, it was during the First and Second Dynasties that the pharaohs and nobles of Egypt began to construct the type of tomb called the "mastaba." The First and Second Dynasties lasted from about 3100 until 2665 BCE. *Mastaba*, by the way, comes from an Arabic word meaning "bench" or "long seat." A mastaba looked like a low, flat-topped rectangle—something like a low bench or a shoebox. Essentially, the pointed pyramid was no more than an extension upward of the flat-topped mastaba.

Mentor

5. *Look at number five. Which word or words are in your notes? They were all related to the definition of* mastaba, *but* a, *bench, is the meaning of the related word in Arabic. And* b, *shoebox, is something the lecturer compared a* mastaba *to, to give you a better idea what it might look like. These words are not as important as the words at* c *and* d*—flat and rectangle—that describe the special shape of a* mastaba. *If you wrote either "low and flat" or "rectangle," that's fine. If you wrote both in your notes, that's excellent. My note is* c.

Part 3

Lecturer: The first "typical" pyramid—or at least what most people generally think a pyramid looks like—was built during the Third Dynasty, which lasted roughly from about 2664 until 2615 BCE. This pyramid was built for King Zoser—that's spelled *Z-o-s-e-r*—in about 2650 BCE. It was built by an architect named Imhotep—*I-m-h-o-t-e-p*. This pyramid was constructed as a series of giant steps. It, along with others of its type, is called a step pyramid.

It was really simply a pile of mastabas, each step smaller and higher than the one before.

Mentor

6. *Look at number six. Which is similar to your notes:* a, b, *or* c?

Let's look at the notes in c *first. The notetaker did not use many abbreviations or symbols. This is not good because it takes too long to write out all the words in a sentence. You might miss an important point in the lecture. It's better to use symbols and abbreviations and write short notes, like those in* a *and* b.

Notes a, b, *and* c *all record the names* Zoser *and* Imhotep. *That's good! The lecturer spelled these names, so you know they are important. Notetaker* c *didn't catch the full spelling of* Imhotep *but left space for it. If this happens to you, you can leave a space and after class ask the professor or a classmate for the missing information.*

My notes are b. *Notice I put a little drawing in my notes. Sometimes a drawing can help you more than just words when you review your notes later.*

Remember to leave space in your notes. After the lecture, you can go back and write in more detail.

ACCURACY CHECK Page 30

1. How many consecutive dynasties ruled ancient Egypt?
2. What was the main purpose of the pyramids?
3. What is *not* an example of "grave goods" that the Egyptians provided for a dead person to take to the next world?
4. What was the first type of pyramid called?
5. Where are the three Great Pyramids located?
6. What did the ancient Greeks call King Khufu?
7. What was the approximate number of the limestone blocks that were used to build Khufu's pyramid?
8. How was King Thutmose I's tomb different from the tombs of previous pharaohs?

CHAPTER 4

The First Emperor of China: Building an Empire and a House of Eternity

VOCABULARY PREVIEW Page 34

A

1. Archaeologists find out about these ancient times by studying the ruins of cities, monuments, or tombs, or any written records that remain.
2. The history part of my talk will be about Qin Shi Huang, who was the founder of the first unified empire in China.
3. Today, I'm also going to be talking about what has been found, to date, in the area of Qin Shi Huang's tomb.
4. Before Qin Shi Huang unified the empire in 221 BCE, China had been torn apart by wars between seven regional kingdoms.
5. When Qin Shi Huang became Emperor, he decreed that a standardized system of Chinese characters was to be used throughout the empire.
6. In the second year after unification, construction of three major imperial highways was begun.
7. At this point, I'm going to segue from talking about the biography of Qin Shi Huang to the archaeology part of my lecture.
8. It seems that as soon as the Emperor gained power, he became preoccupied with death, and with constructing a magnificent House of Eternity for his afterlife.
9. The entire area of the tomb covers approximately 56.25 square kilometers.
10. It is even believed that mercury was pumped through the tomb to create the image of flowing rivers in the tomb area.
11. Without a doubt, the most striking features of the Emperor's House of Eternity are the terra-cotta warriors and horses found in the tomb area.
12. Chinese officials say that the tomb mound of the first Chinese emperor will not be excavated until preservation techniques have advanced significantly.

NOTETAKING PREPARATION Page 35

B

Lecturer: Qin Shi Huang did a number of things to unify and protect his empire. First, he standardized the system for writing Chinese characters. Prior to his unification of the empire, the writing of Chinese characters varied in the different kingdoms. Qin, however, decreed that a standardized system of Chinese characters be used throughout the empire. Next, he decreed that there would be just one system of weights and measures and one system of currency, rather than many different systems, as had been the case before unification. To protect his new empire from the barbarian tribes to the north, he ordered the construction of the Great Wall of China.

FIRST LISTENING Page 36

Lecturer: The fields of history and archaeology go hand in hand. Let me explain what I mean. History is often the story of a particular person, a person like the Emperor

Napoleon. Or, history is the story of a nation, such as the country of France. On the other hand, archaeology is the study of the people, the customs, and the life of ancient times. Archaeologists find out about these ancient times by studying the ruins of cities, monuments, or tombs, or any written records that remain.

In today's lecture I'm going to talk a little about a particular person in ancient Chinese history, and I'm also going to talk about one of the greatest archaeological discoveries of the late twentieth century. The history part of my talk will be about Qin Shi Huang, who was the founder of the first unified empire in China. He lived between 259 BCE. and 210 BCE, and he is often called the First Emperor of China. Just as the exploits of the Emperor Napoleon still fascinate many people and scholars today, so does the story of Qin Shi Huang and his house of eternity. Today, I'm also going to be talking about what has been found, to date, in the area of Qin Shi Huang's tomb. We don't know what additional treasures of Chinese history and culture will be found in the tomb area in the future, but what has been discovered so far is an incredible find for Chinese archaeology and ancient history.

To set the historical context for the excavation of Qin Shi Huang's House of Eternity, I'd like to first talk a little bit about the man himself. His name was Ying Zheng and he was the king of Qin, one of seven regional kingdoms. He took the title Qin Si Huang Di when he became Emperor. Before Qin Si Huang unified the empire in 221 BCE, China had been torn apart by wars between its seven regional kingdoms. Qin defeated the other six kingdoms. Qin's defeat of the other six kingdoms accomplished two things: First, it ended the power of these other six kingdoms. Second, the unification of the seven kingdoms started a centralized imperial system that lasted more than 2,000 years.

Qin Shi Huang did a number of things to unify and protect his empire. First, he standardized the system for writing Chinese characters. Prior to his unification of the empire, the writing of Chinese characters varied in the different kingdoms. Qin, however, decreed that a standardized system of Chinese characters be used throughout the empire. Next, he decreed that there would be just one system of weights and measures and one system of currency, rather than many different systems, as had been the case before unification. To protect his new empire from the barbarian tribes to the north, he ordered the construction of the Great Wall of China.

Now, there already were small walls scattered across the northwest frontier of the empire, but Qin Shi Huang had these walls joined together to create 1,500 miles of fortification and protection for his empire. Qin Shi Huang also began an enormous road-building project. In the second year after unification, construction of three major imperial highways was begun. These highways eventually stretched approximately 6,800 kilometers, or 4,225 miles, throughout the empire. Just in comparison, by the year 150 CE the Roman Empire's road system was about 5,984 kilometers, or 3,718 miles. The Roman Empire's system stretched all the way from Scotland to Rome and then to Jerusalem.

Qin Shi Huang also began another large construction project—the building of his tomb, or mausoleum. It seems that as soon as the Emperor gained power, he became preoccupied with death and with constructing a magnificent House of Eternity for his afterlife. At this point, I'm going to segue from the biography of Qin Shi Huang to the archaeology part of my lecture. Let's see. OK. As I mentioned, when Qin Shi Huang became emperor, he immediately began construction of his House of Eternity. And what an incredible House of Eternity it was! Archaeologists believe that 700,000 laborers were forced to work on the tomb for about 11 years. The entire area of the tomb covers approximately 56.25 square kilometers. It is believed that the tomb was intended to be a microcosmic replica of the Qin capital around the years 221 to 210 BCE. Archaeologists also believe that Qin Shi Huang's tomb contained imperial palaces filled with rare gems and other treasures, and that it also contained gardens and temples. It is even believed that mercury was pumped through the tomb to create the image of flowing rivers in the tomb area. Can you imagine rivers of mercury in a tomb? A 12,000-square-meter area at the site of the tomb has a very high mercury content—in fact, 10 times higher than that of the surrounding area, so archaeologists think that it is very likely that the mercury rivers did, indeed, flow through the tomb area.

Without a doubt, the most striking features of the Qin's House of Eternity are the terra-cotta warriors and horses found in the tomb area. In 1975, Chinese authorities built a museum on the excavation site to preserve these terra-cotta warriors and horses and the other incredible treasures that were being uncovered. Today, the museum covers an area of 16,300 square meters. That means the area is more than two football fields long! The area is divided into three sections, or what are called pits: Number 1 Pit, Number 2 Pit, and Number 3 Pit. Number 1 Pit is the largest of the three pits; it's approximately 960 square meters in size. It first opened to the public on China's National Day in 1979. In Number 1 Pit, there are columns of soldiers at the front, followed by war chariots at the back. It is estimated that there are 3,210 terra-cotta foot soldiers in this pit alone. In 1976, Number 2 Pit was unearthed. It contained nearly a thousand warriors and 90 wooden chariots. This pit was opened to the public in 1994, and today visitors from all over the world go to see Qin Shi Huang's House of Eternity, and to see his terra-cotta army that was to protect his tomb. Altogether more than 7,000 terra-cotta soldiers, horses, chariots, and even weapons have been found in these three pits, and more will likely be found in the future as archaeologists continue to explore and excavate the tomb area.

I'd like to finish up my talk by referencing what Peter Hessler in *National Geographic Magazine* says about the ancient Chinese emperors' view of the afterlife. Mr. Hessler says that the emperors of ancient China saw the afterlife as a continuation of life on earth, much as the ancient Egyptians did. He also notes that archaeologists working on the tomb of the First Emperor of China are "dusting off a window to the past." They're dusting off this window to give us a vision of what mattered to the ancient rulers and their cultures. We have much more to learn from the tomb of the First Emperor of China as excavation of the tomb area continues. We don't know when the excavation will be complete. Chinese officials say that the tomb mound of the first Chinese emperor will not be excavated until preservation techniques have advanced significantly.

Well, that's about all I have to say for today. See you next time.

SECOND LISTENING Page 38

See First Listening, above.

THIRD LISTENING Page 38

Part 1

Lecturer: To protect his new empire from the barbarian tribes to the north, he ordered the construction of the Great Wall of China.

Now, there already were small walls scattered across the northwest frontier of the empire, but Qin Shi Huang had these walls joined together to create 1,500 miles of fortification and protection for his empire. Qin Shi Huang also began an enormous road-building project.

Mentor

1. *Look at number one. Which is similar to your notes,* a *or* b*?*

   The notes in a *are long. There are no abbreviations; this is not good. It takes too long to write out all the words in a sentence. It's better to write short notes, like the ones in* b*. My notes are* b.

   Let's look at b*. Space is used here to show the relationship between ideas. Both the Great Wall and the roads were related to the idea of protecting the empire. The notes in* a *do not show that relationship. The notes in* b *show it clearly because those two points are indented.*

   Notetaker a *recorded both the kilometers and the miles for the highways. It isn't necessary to write both. In* b *I wrote the first number, the kilometers. I didn't write its equivalent in miles as well.*

Part 2

Lecturer: In the second year after unification, construction of three major imperial highways was begun. These highways eventually stretched approximately 6,800 kilometers, or 4,225 miles, throughout the empire. Just in comparison, by the year 150 CE the Roman Empire's road system was about 5,984 kilometers, or 3,718 miles. The Roman Empire's system stretched all the way from Scotland to Rome and then to Jerusalem.

Mentor

2. *Now look at number two. Circle the one that looks like your notes.*

   Notetaker b *recorded both the kilometers and the miles for the highways. It isn't necessary to write both. My notes are* a*. I recorded the first number, the kilometers. I didn't write its equivalent in miles as well.*

   Before the lecturer gave the information about the Roman roads he said, "Just in comparison." This means it is for your information. The important point is that the highways were more extensive than the Roman roads. The exact difference is not important, so in a *I did not write down that information.*

Part 3

Lecturer: Qin Shi Huang also began another large construction project—the building of his tomb, or mausoleum. It seems that as soon as the Emperor gained power, he became preoccupied with death, and with constructing a magnificent House of Eternity for his afterlife. At this point, I'm going to segue from the biography of Qin Shi Huang to the archaeology part of my lecture. Let's see. OK. As I mentioned, when Qin Shi Huang became emperor, he immediately began construction of his House of Eternity. And what an incredible House of Eternity it was!

Mentor

3. *Look at number three. Were your notes similar to* a, b, *or* c*?*

   If your notes are like a, *you noted the transition from the biography part of the lecture to the archaeology part with an arrow. This is OK, but it is clearer to show a change in topic by leaving space between them.*

   I wrote the notes in c*. I left space to show that this was the second part of the lecture.*

   If your notes are like those in b, *you may be confused when you go back and look at your notes, because they don't show the lecturer's shift in focus.*

ACCURACY CHECK Page 39

1. When was Qin Shi Huang born?
2. In what year did Qin Shi Huang unify the empire in China?
3. Why did Qin Shi Huang build the Great Wall of China?

4. How long is the Great Wall of China?
5. How many kilometers of highway were built in Qin Shi Huang's reign?
6. How long did construction of the emperor's tomb take?
7. How large was the tomb?
8. What did archaeologists find traces of in the excavation site?

UNIT 3

Sociology: The Changing World of Work

CHAPTER 5

The Distributed Workforce: Where and When People Work

VOCABULARY PREVIEW Page 47

A

1. Employees may be based in a traditional office setting; or they might work from home—so-called telecommuters; or they could be mobile employees, such as salespeople.
2. Employees working outside of the office need access from remote locations to company servers and to stay connected with the use of cellular technology.
3. Full-time employees often expect benefits such as health insurance, and they might be difficult to terminate.
4. It is not yet understood what impact a distributed workforce is having on the intangible yet vital development of a business culture.
5. How can group cohesion be developed and maintained when face-to-face meetings are rare or nonexistent?
6. How dependent are qualities such as loyalty and ethical behavior on personal relationships that are established through face-to-face contact?
7. Can personal relationships truly evolve across a distributed workforce, where much of the work is conducted in a virtual rather than physical environment?
8. When workers are available 24–7, it can lead to a blurring of the line between work and personal life.
9. In a wired world, there is no downtime.
10. Since the Industrial Revolution, the workplace has been where a large proportion of the adult population spends much of its time.

NOTETAKING PREPARATION Page 48

A

Lecturer

1. But with temporary employees, businesses can easily expand or contract their workforce in reaction to changing market demands. And what . . .
2. They work for themselves, and so have more control over their work schedules and the quality of their work lives than more traditional employees.
   Well, now . . .
3. Technology that enables workers to perform their duties from any location with an Internet connection makes it possible for the work to come to the worker, rather than requiring the worker to go where the jobs are. Being able . . .

B

Lecturer

1. But with temporary employees, businesses can easily expand or contract their workforce in reaction to changing market demands. And what are the benefits to workers?
2. They work for themselves, and so have more control over their work schedules and the quality of their work lives than more traditional employees.
   Well, now let's turn to the challenges and potential disadvantages—for both business and workers—of a distributed workforce.
3. Technology that enables workers to perform their duties from any location with an Internet connection makes it possible for the work to come to the worker, rather than requiring the worker to go where the jobs are. Being able to get a job without relocating allows a worker with the skills a business needs to stay close to family and friends, even when the local economy is weak.

FIRST LISTENING Page 49

Lecturer: For many years, people working in offices—often referred to as "white-collar" workers—have gone "to the office" to work. For them, going to work and going to the office meant the same thing. You got up, you left your home, and you went "to work." You went to your employer's office. You did your job, and at the end of the workday, you left and perhaps didn't think about work until the next working day. But nowadays, we live in a 24–7, globally connected world. Business is always underway, if not in your own time zone then in another one. Increasingly, there is no "end of the workday."

So today we are going to be talking about an important trend in the evolution of work, a trend brought about by rapid technological change and globalization: the growth of the distributed workforce.

First of all, a definition: A *distributed workforce* is a workforce that is not located in one geographic location. Rather, the workforce is distributed across sometimes quite large geographic areas, and working arrangements and terms of employment are quite diverse. Businesses with a distributed workforce have employees working in various locations—in different parts of a country, or increasingly, in different countries. Employees can be employed under a variety of working arrangements. They may be based in a traditional office setting; they might work from home—so-called telecommuters who are rarely in the office; they could be mobile employees, such as salespeople, who report in from the field; or they might be temporary or contract workers, hired only for a specific project. These are just a few possible working arrangements. OK. So, a distributed workforce is one that is distributed geographically and works under a variety of arrangements, some traditional, such as full-time employees based at a company office, and others far less traditional, such as employees who work from a distant location without ever setting foot in an office.

To the growing number of employers who use a distributed workforce, and to the members of that workforce, technology is absolutely essential. This is because employees working outside of the office need access from remote locations to company servers and also need to stay connected with the use of cellular technology. In fact, it is clear that the ability of businesses to employ a distributed workforce would not be possible without advanced technology—technology that allows work to be conducted in a virtual space that is not bound by geography, set working times, or the need for physical, face-to-face communication.

The ability to utilize a distributed workforce brings many advantages to businesses and workers. But, there are also challenges. So let's look at some of the advantages and disadvantages, and consider the impact on workers, employers, and the larger society.

First, the advantages. The benefits of a distributed workforce to a global business are pretty obvious: If the business is global, having a workforce positioned in the countries where that business is conducted is an obvious advantage. A local workforce will understand the local cultural and business norms.

A second benefit is flexibility. Employment policies and conditions can be determined by local standards and can vary from location to location. For example, an American-based business might employ software engineers in India at lower pay than engineers with similar qualifications in the United States would expect. Or, a company might hire temporary employees and consultants rather than taking on new, full-time employees. Full-time employees often expect benefits and—depending on local labor laws—might be difficult to terminate. But with temporary employees, businesses can easily expand or contract their workforce in reaction to changing market demands.

And what are the benefits to workers? Technology that enables workers to perform their duties from any location with an Internet connection makes it possible for the work to come to the worker, rather than requiring the worker to go where the jobs are. Being able to get a job without relocating allows a worker with the skills a business needs to stay close to family and friends, even when the local economy is weak. So workers performing tasks that, thanks to technology, no longer require their physical presence at a particular location can benefit from being members of a distributed workforce. In addition, there are those workers who are independent contractors or consultants. They work for themselves, and so have more control over their work schedules and the quality of their work lives than more traditional employees.

Well, now let's turn to the challenges and potential disadvantages—for both business and workers—of a distributed workforce. One of the major business challenges is not yet fully understood: the impact a distributed workforce is having on the intangible, yet vital development and maintenance of a business culture. For example, how can group cohesion be developed and maintained when face-to-face meetings are rare or nonexistent? How is a corporate culture established and passed on when most communications take place online? What about qualities such as loyalty and ethical behavior? How dependent are these qualities on personal relationships established through face-to-face contact? Can they truly evolve across a distributed workforce, where much of the work is conducted in a virtual, rather than physical environment? Such questions about the establishment and maintenance of group cohesion, corporate culture, group loyalty, and ethical behavior are critical; no one knows the answers, but one thing is clear: The technology that is driving this evolution in the nature of work is already here, and it's here to stay.

On the other hand, the disadvantages for the workers are more tangible. For one, the technology allows, encourages, and sometimes requires workers to be available 24–7. This can lead to a blurring of the line between work and personal life, which many studies show leads to a great deal of stress. In a wired world, there is no downtime. So, even though working in your pajamas from home might sound like the height of freedom and relaxation, the reality can be quite different. Even if you are in your pajamas, being unable to disconnect from work might begin to feel even more confining than reporting to the office wearing a suit and tie for a limited amount of time a week.

Another disadvantage for workers is that, although some work arrangements can give welcome flexibility, this flexibility comes at a cost—job security. Temporary employees and consultants have little or no job security; because they are self-employed, they are usually not protected from sudden termination by local labor laws. In addition, they rarely receive benefits such as health insurance and paid vacation. Finally, some early studies on telecommuting revealed that telecommuters work longer hours for less pay than office-based workers. Preliminary studies show that many of the benefits associated with telecommuting—primarily of cost savings—benefit employers, rather than workers.

Now, what about the impact on the larger society? People are social beings. And since the Industrial Revolution, the workplace has been where a large proportion of the adult population spends much of its time, interacting in a complex social environment. Work is a highly organized social experience, with many daily opportunities for face-to-face communication. While it is still far too early to say what impact the disappearance of a physical workplace for a significant proportion of the population might have on the larger society, there seems little doubt that it will have an impact.

Distance workers say they feel the loss of the informal social networks that exist in an office setting; they report feelings of isolation and a lack of support. They now have to establish and maintain informal support networks. In an office, this happened during the course of the workday when getting a coffee with a co-worker or chatting by the copy machine.

There is also concern about the extent to which distance work—telecommuting—has allowed employers to enter the employee's private, family life, and what impact this blurring of private life and work life might have. While telecommuting is often promoted as a way for people to balance home and work more efficiently, the reality is less clear. As I mentioned earlier, although many telecommuters have the advantage of being able to set their own schedules, freeing up time during the day to attend to family responsibilities, this flexibility often means putting in extra hours in the evening and on weekends, time that used to be reserved for private life.

So to recap, we have discussed one aspect of how the nature of work is evolving due to rapid technological change and globalization: the growth of a distributed workforce. You heard about some of the advantages and disadvantages for both employers and workers, as well as the potential impact on society. And in fact many questions about the impact that these changes are having on our society remain unanswered. But, I'm afraid that's all we have time for today.

SECOND LISTENING Page 51

See First Listening, above.

THIRD LISTENING Page 51

Part 1

Lecturer: And what are the benefits to workers? Technology that enables workers to perform their duties from any location with an Internet connection makes it possible for the work to come to the worker, rather than requiring the worker to go where the jobs are. Being able to get a job without relocating allows a worker with the skills a business needs to stay close to family and friends, even when the local economy is weak. So workers performing tasks that, thanks to technology, no longer require their physical presence at a particular location can benefit from being members of a distributed workforce. In addition, there are those workers who are independent contractors or consultants. They work for themselves, and so have more control over their work schedules and the quality of their work lives than more traditional employees.

Mentor

1. *Look at number one. Which notes look most like yours?*

In both a *and* b, *the stressed word* workers *is clearly recorded.*

The word benefits *was not stressed, but is important to your understanding of this part of the lecture. Both* a *and* b *recorded this, in their notes, but* a *used the symbol "++" meaning good or positive things, and* b *wrote out the word. It's more efficient to use symbols as in* a, *but the notes in* b *are also clear, which is the most important thing.*

Look at a *again. There are two benefits listed. Now look at* b. *In* b *there are three. The first and second are not separate advantages. The fact that workers can stay close to family and friends is an example, not a separate main point. The lecturer did not use strong downward intonation, a long pause, or a signal word at this point.*

My notes are in a.

Part 2

Lecturer: Distance workers say they feel the loss of the informal social networks that exist in an office setting; they report feelings of isolation and a lack of support. They now have to establish and maintain informal support networks. In an office, this happened during the course of the workday, when getting a coffee with a co-worker or chatting by the copy machine.

There is also concern about the extent to which distance work—telecommuting—has allowed employers to enter the employee's private, family life, and what impact this blurring of private life and work life might have. While telecommuting is often promoted as a way for people to balance home and work more efficiently, the reality is less clear. As I mentioned earlier, although many telecommuters have the advantage of being able to set their own schedules, freeing up time during the day to attend to family responsibilities, this flexibility often means putting in extra hours in the evening and on weekends, time that used to be reserved for private life.

Mentor

2. *Look at number two. Which heading most accurately reflects the key point of this part of the lecture— "distance workers" as in* a, *or "office workers" as in* b, *or "informal support networks" as in* c?

   The heading "distance workers" in a *is best. The speaker deals specifically with just one type of working arrangement, that of the distance worker.*

   My notes are a.

3. *Now look at number three. Which notes are most like yours?*

   In a, *two main points are recorded. This is correct. There was only one place where intonation, pause, and signal word indicated the speaker had concluded one main point and was moving on to another: the strong rise and fall intonation on the words* copy machine *followed by a marked pause and the signal word* also.

   Look at b *and* c. *In* b *there are four main points, and in* c *there are three. In both, support for the main points is confused with the points themselves.*

   In b, *notes 1 and 2 could be combined, as in* a. *Notes 3 and 4 could also be combined.*

   In c, *note 3 is detailed information that supports note 2, not a new main point.*

   My notes are a.

Part 3

Lecturer: Another disadvantage for workers is that, although some work arrangements can give welcome flexibility, this flexibility comes at a cost—job security. Temporary employees and consultants have little or no job security; because they are self-employed, they are usually not protected from sudden termination by local labor laws. In addition, they rarely receive benefits such as health insurance and paid vacation. Finally, some early studies on telecommuting revealed that telecommuters work longer hours for less pay than office-based workers.

Mentor

4. *Now look at number four. Which notes are most like yours? My notes are* b.

   Both a *and* b *use a heading, which is good. The heading in* b *is clear and accurate. The heading in* a *is confusing. The focus in this part of the lecture is disadvantages for workers, not flexibility. Flexibility is an advantage.*

   In both a *and* b *the first note is "job security." In* b, *the minus symbol makes it clear this is a lack of job security—a disadvantage. In* a, *the first note could be interpreted as an advantage instead of a disadvantage when the notes are reviewed later.*

   The notes in a *show two main points; the notes in* b *show three. Three, as in* b, *is correct because the information about benefits is a new main point. In* a, *the information about benefits is recorded as part of the first main point. The notetaker for* a *did not notice the intonation, pause, and signal word indicating a new main point.*

ACCURACY CHECK Page 52

1. How does the lecturer describe a white-collar worker?
2. What has brought about the growth of the distributed workforce?
3. What is true of a distributed workforce?
4. What was *not* mentioned in the lecture as a benefit to employers of a distributed workforce?
5. What was *not* mentioned in the lecture as a benefit to employees of a distributed workforce?
6. For employers, what is a disadvantage of having a distributed workforce?
7. For employees, what is a disadvantage of being part of distributed workforce?
8. What is one potential impact on society of the growth of a distributed workforce?

CHAPTER 6

Age and Work: The Graying of the Workforce

VOCABULARY PREVIEW Page 56

A

1. The human lifespan is also increasing: the National Institute on Aging reports that most countries show a steady increase in longevity.
2. A falling birthrate in countries with advanced economies has contributed to a rapid increase in the age of the world's population.
3. The reasons for the declining birthrate require a bit of explanation.
4. The need for cheap labor to work the land, coupled with high infant mortality, made large families advantageous.
5. During industrialization, there was a population shift from rural to urban areas.
6. Advances in reproductive technology allowed couples to take a more active role in planning their families.
7. In many developed nations, the birthrate has now fallen to below replacement levels.

8. The fertility rate in many European countries is now less than 1.5 children per woman.
9. The elderly support ratio is calculated by dividing the number of working-age people by the number of people 65 or older.
10. A second impact is caused by just the opposite phenomenon, the large number of baby boomers who are and will be retiring at the same time, taking with them knowledge and expertise that will be difficult to replace over the short term.
11. Clashes can occur when workers with such widely different life experiences and attitudes toward work interact.
12. Some companies have had to scale back expansion due to a lack of workers.

NOTETAKING PREPARATION Page 57

B

1. And despite its large population, China's fertility rate is just 1.5, a result of government policies to limit families to just one child.
2. In fact, some companies have had to scale back expansion due to a lack of the highly skilled workers such expansion depends on.

FIRST LISTENING Page 58

Lecturer: Last time, we discussed one of the ways that the world of work has been changing: the growth of the distributed workforce. Today, we are going to talk about a change in the world of work that has been brought about by changes in the makeup of the population of the workforce. What I am talking about is the aging, or as some refer to it, the graying, of the workforce.

First, some population statistics and predictions: According to the World Health Organization, the number of people today who are aged 60 and over has doubled since 1980. It is projected that within the next five years, for the first time in history the number of adults aged 65 and over will outnumber children under the age of 5. By 2050, these older adults will outnumber all children under the age of 14. And, the human lifespan is also increasing: the National Institute on Aging reports that most countries, including developing countries, show a steady increase in longevity.

So . . . what does all of this have to do with work? The answer to that is the subject of today's lecture. First, I will explain some historical factors that have contributed to the rapid aging of the human population. I will then move on to the main point of the lecture—that is, the impact that this aging population is having on the world of work.

Now . . . how did we get to be so old? Two basic trends have resulted in the rapid increase in the age of the world's population: a falling birthrate in countries with advanced economies, and improvements in medical care that have contributed to an increased lifespan. Medical advances are easy enough to understand, but the reasons for the declining birthrate require a bit of explanation.

Prior to the Industrial Revolution, much of the population grew their own food on small farms. Therefore, large families were an advantage—the need for cheap labor to work the land, coupled with high infant mortality, made large families advantageous. During industrialization, there was a population shift from rural to urban areas, where factories were located. As a result of this shift, the need for large families began to decline. This, combined with advances in reproductive technology that allowed couples to take a more active role in planning their families, led to a gradual decline in the birthrate. By the start of World War II, in parts of Europe and the United States the birthrate had fallen close to replacement levels—that is, the level at which the number of babies being born is roughly equivalent to the number of people dying.

This trend, however, was interrupted by what has come to be known as the baby boom—the period of time following World War II—1946 to 1964—when birthrates increased sharply. This sudden and unexpected rise in the birthrate was only temporary, however; by the mid-1960s it had fallen to pre–World War II levels. And it has continued to fall ever since. Globally, since the early 1970s the population growth rate has fallen by more than 40 percent. And in many developed nations, the birthrate has now fallen to below replacement levels. The fertility rate in many European countries is now less than 1.5 children per woman, which is far below the replacement rate of 2.1. In Japan the rate is just 1.4, and the lowest fertility rate is South Korea's, at 1.2 children per woman. And despite its large population, China's fertility rate is just 1.5, a result of government policies to limit families to just one child.

If this global trend toward fewer children continues, it will have an enormous impact on society's ability to support its growing number of elderly citizens. And that brings us back to our topic today—the impact of an aging population on the world of work.

To understand the profound impact of rising life expectancy and falling birthrate, you need to understand the elderly support ratio. The elderly support ratio is calculated by dividing the number of working-age people—ages 15 to 64—by the number of people 65 or older. This ratio gives a rough idea of how many support providers are available for each elderly person who might be dependent on the work of others. To give you an indication of the enormous change that is taking place: According to the Population Research Bureau, in 1950 there were 12 working-age people for every elderly person in the world; by 2010, this ratio had declined to 9. The ratio actually varies significantly from country to country, with the lowest ratios being in the advanced economies of the developed world. To put this into perspective, in Europe today there are fewer than 5 working-age people to support each elderly person; in Japan, Italy, and Germany, the ratio is even lower—only 3. By 2050, projections indicate that the ratio for the world will decline from 9 working adults per elderly person to 4, with Japan having the lowest ratio of just 1 to 1.

The potential impact on the world of work is profound. One result is the number of older workers who are now remaining in their jobs past retirement age. A second impact is caused by just the opposite phenomenon, the large number of baby boomers who are and will be retiring at the same time, taking with them knowledge and expertise that will be difficult to replace over the short term. OK, let's address each of these in turn.

First of all, the fact that a large number of baby boomers at or nearing retirement age are remaining in their jobs means that young workers entering the workforce are finding it difficult to find work, particularly in desirable, white-collar, professional jobs. According to the U.S. Bureau of Labor Statistics, the median age of the American worker has risen dramatically in recent years—from 35 in 1980 to 42 in 2010. And at the executive level, the median age is quite a bit higher, at about 52.

Globally, 14 percent of the workforce is now over the age of 55, but according to the McKinsey Global Institute, that figure will rise to 22 percent by 2030. In the past, older workers retired (or died), so at any one time there might have been two generations in the workforce at the same time. Now, the workplace has become increasingly multigenerational, with young, middle-aged, and older workers.

When younger people do find work, they will often encounter co-workers who are two to three generations older than they are. This generation gap is made even wider by the so-called digital divide, that is, the quite different levels of comfort with technology between "digital natives"—young people who have never known anything but a wireless, connected world—and aging baby boomers who grew up without personal computers, much less social networking. In today's working world, management is increasingly having to deal with the inevitable clashes that can occur when workers with such widely different life experiences and attitudes toward work interact.

Now, the other trend affecting the world of work is directly related to the fact that all these baby boomers are nearing retirement age at the same time. While some are remaining on the job, as we have just discussed, many are leaving the workforce and retiring, taking with them the experience and knowledge gained over long careers, often spent working for the same company. This expertise is not easily replaced in younger workers who have little to no experience or change jobs frequently and lack the institutional knowledge of the baby boomers. The loss of highly skilled employees—those whose jobs involve interaction between two people and which require problem-solving skills and experience, such as engineers, nurses, and lawyers—is in turn affecting the productivity of many companies. In fact, some companies have had to scale back expansion due to a lack of the highly skilled workers such expansion depends on.

And, if population growth in advanced economies such as Japan and much of Europe remains low, this problem will persist far beyond the retirement of the baby boomers—there will simply not be enough young workers to replace retirees. Although in the short term it might seem that older workers are standing in the way of younger workers seeking employment, over the long term the labor of older workers will be essential to economic growth. In addition, as the human lifespan increases, people will need to work longer to make enough money to support themselves in an old age that could last quite a bit longer than it did in previous generations. And, with a longer working life and rapid changes brought about by technology, the idea of having just one career is likely to be a thing of the past. Instead, most people will be having second and even third careers—with their final career just getting started when they are in their 60s.

At this point, it is unclear how employers and workers themselves will adapt to the need—and often desire—of older people to remain in the workforce. At the moment, workplaces aren't designed to meet the needs of their aging workers very well. In fact, cases of age-related discrimination in work are on the rise; companies often lay off their older, more expensive employees first, and in our youth-oriented culture, companies that are hiring often prefer younger candidates, even with far less experience. Clearly, as the population continues to age and remain healthy for a longer period of time, such a youth orientation in the workplace will need to be rethought.

OK, so that's it for today. Don't forget that next week will be our review session for the final exam, so come prepared with your questions.

SECOND LISTENING Page 60

See First Listening, above.

THIRD LISTENING Page 60

Part 1

Lecturer: Prior to the Industrial Revolution, much of the population grew their own food on small farms. Therefore, large families were an advantage—the need for cheap labor to work the land, coupled with high infant mortality, made large families advantageous.

Mentor

1. *Look at number one. Which notes are similar to your notes? Did you notice the cause and effect relationship in this part of the lecture?*

   All three sets of notes list the two reasons the lecturer gave for why having a large family was an advantage before the Industrial Revolution, but they do not all accurately show the cause and effect relationship between those reasons and large families.

   The notes in a *show the time period—before the Industrial Revolution—and the symbol for* because—b/c*—is followed by the two reasons. My notes are* a.

   Now look at b. *In the heading, the arrow pointing left suggests that the time period before the Industrial Revolution was the cause and large families having an advantage was the effect. Also, it is not clear how points 1 and 2 are related to the heading.*

   Now look at c. *In* c, *the Industrial Revolution appears to be the cause of large families, which is not accurate. In fact, big families* stopped *being an advantage during the Industrial Revolution. The time period referred to in this section was* before *the Industrial Revolution.*

Part 2

Lecturer: During industrialization, there was a population shift from rural to urban areas, where factories were located. As a result of this shift, the need for large families began to decline. This, combined with advances in reproductive technology that allowed couples to take a more active role in planning their families, led to a gradual decline in the birthrate.

Mentor

2. *Now look at number two. There were several cues for cause and effect in this part of the lecture:* as a result, allowed, *and* led to. *There was also an implied cause and effect—the idea that the population shift was a result of industrialization. Which notes accurately reflect the causes and effects introduced in this part of the lecture?*

   Both a *and* b *show that industrialization led to a population shift and that the population shift led to a decline in the need for large families. But look at* a. *Do you see what is missing? The move from rural to urban areas was important information that should have been included—as it was in* b.

   In a, *the next point is about reproductive technology. But the relationship of this point to the previous one is not clear. Now compare* a *and* b. *In* b, *the "and" symbol makes it clear that this is an additional point.*

   The left-pointing arrow in a *indicates that reproductive technology was the effect and controlling family size was the cause. But the lecturer said just the opposite. The arrow should point right, as in* b.

   One final point about a*: it looks like the decline in the birthrate is a result of controlling family size through advances in reproductive technology—but that was only one reason for the decline in the birthrate. The other reason was the decline in a need for large families. Look at how the spacing makes this much clearer in* b. *My notes are* b.

Part 3

Lecturer: First of all, the fact that a large number of baby boomers at or nearing retirement age are remaining in their jobs means that young workers entering the workforce are finding it difficult to find work, particularly in desirable, white-collar, professional jobs. According to the U.S. Bureau of Labor Statistics, the median age of the American worker has risen dramatically in recent years—from 35 in 1980 to 42 in 2010.

Mentor

3. *Now look at number three. There is just one cause and effect cue in this part of the lecture: the verb* means. *Both notes* a *and* b *show just one cause and effect relationship.*

   Let's look at a *first. I'm going to "translate"* a, *and you decide if it reflects what the lecturer said. "The American worker's median age rose from 35 in 1980 to 42 in 2010. As a result, young workers are having difficulty finding jobs." Is that right? The lecturer said that baby boomers are working past retirement age—that is important information about cause, but it wasn't included in* a.

   OK, now look at b. *I'm going to "translate" again. "Baby boomers work past retirement age. As a result, young workers have difficulty finding jobs." That makes sense, doesn't it? OK, but there is also an asterisk next to "age" and a note at the bottom of* b. *The note contains the information that the statistics back up the point about retirement age; they show that the median age of American workers is going up. The notes in* b *are mine.*

ACCURACY CHECK Page 61

1. According to the World Health Organization, when will the number of older adults worldwide be higher than the number of children aged 14 and younger?
2. What was true about families before the Industrial Revolution?
3. What is one trend that has contributed to a rapid increase in the age of the world's population?
4. When was the baby boom?
5. Which country has the lowest fertility rate today?
6. Which country is projected to have the lowest elderly support ratio by 2050?
7. What percentage of the global workforce is currently over the age of 55?
8. If population growth remains low in advanced economies, what problem could occur?

UNIT 4

Communication: The Influence of Language, Culture, and Gender

CHAPTER 7

Classroom Communication: Language and Culture in the Classroom

VOCABULARY PREVIEW Page 69

A

1. Communication can take the form of talk, or it can take the form of gestures, or nonverbal signals of one kind or another.
2. Many scholars study the topic of communication in general, and speech communication specifically, in order to learn how individuals send and interpret messages.
3. One area of research in intercultural communication is the study of the influence of the setting, or environment, on the success or failure of communication.
4. When you are asked to picture a classroom in your mind's eye, what do you see?
5. The "classroom" as we know it, by the way, is a relatively recent innovation.
6. In particular, culture influences the rituals that take place in the classroom setting, and the ways that students participate in the classroom discourse.
7. Rituals are systematic procedures used to perform a certain act or to communicate a certain message.
8. In some graduate-level seminars in American universities, students do not make any physical signs when they want to speak; they state their ideas whenever they feel the urge.
9. North American students from families of European origin are usually more talkative in class and more willing to state their opinions than are students of American Indian heritage or from Asian backgrounds.
10. The esteem in which teachers are held also varies from culture to culture.

NOTETAKING PREPARATION Page 70

B

Lecturer: Today's lecture deals with language, culture, and communication in classrooms. First of all, what exactly is communication? One definition is that communication is a form of human behavior that results from a need to interact with other human beings. So, to meet this need, we send verbal and nonverbal messages to communicate with both friends and strangers. Communication can take the form of talk, or it can take the form of gestures, or nonverbal signals, of one kind or another. The talk or signals send messages that communicate a person's thoughts, feelings, and intentions to others.

FIRST LISTENING Page 71

Lecturer: Today's lecture deals with language, culture, and communication in classrooms. First of all, what exactly is communication? One definition is that communication is a form of human behavior that results from a need to interact with other human beings. So, to meet this need, we send verbal and nonverbal messages to communicate with both friends and strangers. Communication can take the form of talk, or it can take the form of gestures, or nonverbal signals, of one kind or another. The talk or signals send messages that communicate a person's thoughts, feelings, and intentions to others. Many scholars study the topic of communication, in general, and speech communication, specifically, in order to learn how individuals send and interpret messages. Some of these scholars conduct research on the topic of intercultural communication. That is, they study communication between people from different cultures. One area of research in intercultural communication is the study of the influence of the setting, or environment, on the success or failure of communication. In this lecture, I'll be talking about one specific aspect of intercultural communication; that is, intercultural communication that takes place in the classroom.

But what exactly is a classroom? When you are asked to picture a classroom in your mind's eye, what do you see? You probably see a classroom that is familiar to you and that would be familiar to students from your culture. Not everyone will see the same picture in their minds. Although many people have a similar mental image of a classroom, their culture greatly influences the way they view the teacher–student relationship. And culture also influences how a person understands the ways in which information is taught and learned in the classroom. Culture also plays an important role in determining how teachers and students communicate in the classroom. In this lecture, I'll give you a few examples of some of the ways that culture affects this communication.

The "classroom" as we know it, by the way, is a relatively recent innovation. Great teachers like Socrates, Plato, Aristotle, and Confucius taught without the benefit of a board, desks, and the standard comforts (or discomforts) of a classroom building.

But let me return to the main topic of this lecture—the influence of culture on behavior and communication between teacher and students in the classroom.

If you have come from another culture to study in the United States, you may already have noticed that teachers and students in American schools interact and communicate in the classroom in ways that differ from how teachers and students communicate in your home culture. It's culture that influences and establishes these interactions and communication patterns.

But what do we mean by culture? Of course, *culture* is a term that is used in many different ways. Basically, culture provides us with a system of knowledge that allows us to communicate with others and teaches us how to interpret their verbal and nonverbal behavior. Culture influences and establishes how people interact with one another—or do not interact with one another. In particular, culture influences the rituals that take place in the classroom setting, and it influences the ways that students participate in the classroom discourse. It also influences the esteem in which teachers are held.

Just what exactly are "rituals"? I'll give you a dictionary definition to begin with: *Rituals* are systematic procedures used to perform a certain act or to communicate a certain message. Well, there are many rituals associated with teaching and learning, and with education in general. In some countries, when a teacher enters the classroom, the students ritually stand up. In the United States, a classroom ritual occurs when students raise their hands to signal to the teacher that they know the answer to a question. This hand raising is not a universal classroom ritual to signal intent to answer a question, however. Jamaican students snap or flap their fingers to signal that they want to answer a question. In some college- and graduate-level seminars in American universities, students do not make any physical signs when they want to speak; they state their ideas whenever they feel the urge or when it is appropriate. This sort of classroom behavior is especially confusing to students from cultures in which there are no rituals for attracting the teacher's attention because the student is not expected to participate in the class at all.

This brings us to the issue of classroom participation. North American students from families of European origin are usually more talkative in class and more willing to state their opinions than are students of American Indian heritage or from Asian backgrounds. This difference is directly related to cultural values about learning and education and classroom behavior. European-American students' culture teaches them that learning is shaped and helped by their talk and active engagement in exploring or discussing issues. Some Asian-born and Asian-American students, however, are generally taught that they will learn best by listening to and absorbing the knowledge being given to them by the teacher. So, some cultures do not have a way for students to signal a desire to talk to a teacher; in these cultures, students speak out only after the teacher has spoken to them.

And what about how teachers are treated? How much are they respected? The esteem in which teachers are held also varies from culture to culture. Many Asian peoples see the teacher, the instructor, the professor as the very "symbol" of learning and culture. In Germany, students value the personal opinions of their instructors and it is not customary to disagree with or contradict a teacher during class. Israeli students, on the other hand, might criticize a teacher who they feel is wrong about an issue or who they believe has provided incorrect information.

There are many other ways that culture can affect interaction and communication between teachers and students in the classroom. I've discussed differences in how students get the teacher's attention during class, and I've pointed out the differences in the ways students from various cultures participate and communicate with the teacher during class. From this brief consideration of classroom communication, you should begin to see that learning a language involves more than studying the vocabulary, idioms, and grammar of the language. If you are to succeed in communicating in a second-language classroom, you need to learn not only the language spoken in the classroom, but also the expected procedures of classroom participation and communication—that is, the rituals of language, culture, and communication.

SECOND LISTENING Page 73

See First Listening, above.

THIRD LISTENING Page 73

Part 1

Lecturer: But what do we mean by culture? Of course, *culture* is a term that is used in many different ways. Basically, culture provides us with a system of knowledge that allows us to communicate with others and teaches us how to interpret their verbal and nonverbal behavior. Culture influences and establishes how people interact with one another—or do not interact with one another.

Mentor

1. *Look at number one. Which notes are similar to your notes? Did you notice the rhetorical question and use the symbols* Q *and* A*?*

   All three of the notes use Q *and* A, *which is good. However, in* c *the question is written out exactly as it was spoken. Try to reduce a rhetorical question to its basic meaning, as in* a *and* b.

Although c *accurately reflects the definition of culture from the lecture, too much is written down—there is no need to write down "basic" or "us." If your notes look like* c*, you've got the idea, but you need to put only the most important information in your notes.*

Now let's look at a *and* b*. Which one most clearly shows the definition of culture? In* b *it seems as if the lecturer gave three different definitions of culture—this is confusing. In fact, the lecturer gave just one definition that contained three key points.*

My notes are a*. These notes clearly show one definition of culture that has three parts.*

Part 2

Lecturer: Just what exactly are "rituals?" I'll give you a dictionary definition to begin with: *Rituals* are systematic procedures used to perform a certain act or to communicate a certain message. Well, there are many rituals associated with teaching and learning, and education in general. In some countries, when a teacher enters the classroom, the students ritually stand up.

Mentor

2. *Look at number two. Which notes are similar to your notes?*

   Did you notice the rhetorical question and use the Q *and* A *symbols, as in* a *and* c*? If so, good.*

   Although b *includes all of the information, it is not as clear as* a *or* c*. In* b *the fact that rituals are a main point in the lecture gets lost. And in* b *it is not visually clear that standing up when a teacher comes in the room is an example of a ritual.*

   No example is given in a*. Including the example, as in* c*, makes the somewhat technical definition of rituals easier to understand. The notes in* c *are mine.*

Part 3

Lecturer: And what about how teachers are treated? How much are they respected? The esteem in which teachers are held also varies from culture to culture. Many Asian peoples see the teacher, the instructor, the professor as the very "symbol" of learning and culture. In Germany, students value the personal opinions of their instructors and it is not customary to disagree with or contradict a teacher during class. Israeli students, on the other hand, might criticize a teacher who they feel is wrong about an issue or who they believe has provided incorrect information.

Mentor

3. *Look at number three. Which notes are most like your notes? Let's look at the differences between* a *and* b*.*

   In b *we see two questions. The lecturer did ask two questions, but was it necessary to write down both? Probably not. The important thing to note was the point about respect. But it is OK to include both questions if you have time to record them.*

   Notes a *and* b *contain similar information. But, which notes make the difference between the main points and the supporting details the most clear?*

   The use of bullets and dashes in a *make a clear distinction between the main points and the examples. My notes are* a*.*

ACCURACY CHECK Page 74

1. What does the lecturer say that culture is?
2. What is raising one's hand to get the teacher's attention an example of?
3. Which is a classroom ritual?
4. Students from Asian backgrounds often do what?
5. Which of the following is usually true in classrooms in Asia?
6. Which of the following is true of German classrooms?
7. Which of the following groups would probably feel the most comfortable disagreeing with a teacher during class?
8. Which of the following is *not* discussed in the lecture?

CHAPTER 8

Gender and Communication: Male–Female Conversation as Cross-cultural Communication

VOCABULARY PREVIEW Page 78

A

1. Boys learn to be masculine and girls learn to be feminine as they grow to be men and women.
2. Children learn how to talk to other children or adults, and how to have conversations, not only from their parents, but also from their peers.
3. Deborah Tannen and other researchers on this topic have found that young boys tend to play outside the home rather than in, and they play in large groups that are hierarchically structured.
4. It is by giving orders and making the other boys play by the rules that boys achieve higher and more dominant status in the play group.
5. Boys also achieve status by taking center stage.
6. The boys were making slingshots; the girls were making jewelry.
7. The girls making the rings were more egalitarian.
8. As a result of our cultural upbringing, we learn norms of behavior and patterns of communication that are often gender based, and sometimes gender biased.
9. Well, perhaps it is our social concept of what is feminine and what is masculine that reinforces the

stereotype that women talk more than men, and even causes these different patterns of communication.

10. This means that a Zulu wife must paraphrase and find other ways to say these things.

NOTETAKING PREPARATION Page 79

B

Lecturer: Another well-known researcher, Marjorie Harness Goodwin, compared boys and girls engaged in two task-oriented activities. The boys were making slingshots. The girls were making jewelry; they were making rings for their fingers. Goodwin noted that the boys' activity group was hierarchically arranged. The "leader" told the other boys what to do and how to do it. The girls making the rings were more egalitarian. Everyone made suggestions about how to make the rings, and the girls tended to listen and accept the suggestions of the other girls in the group.

FIRST LISTENING Page 80

Lecturer: In the last lecture, you heard about the relationship between culture and classroom communication. In this lecture, I'll talk about another variable that affects human communication. That variable is gender. Gender is the social identity that men and women learn as they grow up in a culture. For example, boys learn to be "masculine" and girls learn to be "feminine" as they grow to be men and women. Researchers have shown that men and women—and boys and girls, for that matter—communicate in quite different ways and in different amounts, depending on the situation the speakers find themselves in, and the reason or reasons they're communicating with other people.

Many cultures actually encourage men and women to talk differently and in different amounts, and these patterns for communicating are learned when men and women are young boys and girls. Children learn how to talk to other children or adults, and how to have conversations, not only from their parents, but also from their peers—other boys and girls their age. In her best-selling book, *You Just Don't Understand*, Deborah Tannen points out that although American boys and girls often play together, they spend most of their time playing in same-sex groups. She also points out that boys and girls do play some games together, but their favorite games are very often quite different.

Tannen and other researchers on this topic have found that young boys, say ages eight through twelve, tend to play outside the home rather than in, and they play in large groups that are hierarchically structured. The group of boys generally has a leader who tells the other boys what to do and how to do it. It is by giving orders and making the other boys play by the rules that boys achieve higher and more dominant status in the play group. Boys also achieve status by taking "center stage." They take center stage by talking a lot; they give orders and commands; they tell a lot of stories and jokes. They command attention by dominating conversations and by interrupting other boys who are speaking. The researchers also found that boys' games often have clear winners and losers and complicated systems of rules.

Researchers found that girls have their own kinds of games with their own rules. And they follow their own patterns and styles of communication when playing together. Tannen and her colleagues have found that young girls often play in small groups or in pairs. There is little hierarchical order to their group play. In their games, like hopscotch and jump rope, every girl gets a chance to play. Researchers have also found that girls usually don't give many direct orders or commands to their playmates; they express their preferences as suggestions, according to Tannen. In many of their play activities there are no "winners" or "losers."

Girls often say to their playmates, "Let's do" this or that. Boys, on the other hand, are more direct in ordering their playmates to do this or that. Tannen is quick to point out that North American boys as well as girls want to get their way and want other children to do what they want them to do; however, boys and girls try to get their playmates to do what they want them to do in different ways.

Another well-known researcher, Marjorie Harness Goodwin, compared boys and girls engaged in two task-oriented activities. The boys were making slingshots. The girls were making jewelry; they were making rings for their fingers. Goodwin noted that the boys' activity group was hierarchically arranged. The "leader" told the other boys what to do and how to do it. The girls making the rings were more egalitarian. Everyone made suggestions about how to make the rings, and the girls tended to listen and accept the suggestions of the other girls in the group.

Goodwin is not suggesting that girls never engage in some of the communication and management behaviors boys engage in. In fact, in another study, she found that when girls "play house," the girl who plays the mother gives orders to the girls who play the children. But girls seem to give orders to their peers less often than boys do when they play. In the game of playing house, the girls are practicing parent–child relationships. And, it's very likely that when little boys play their games, they are practicing the masculine roles they're expected to assume when they grow up.

So. As a result of our cultural upbringing, we learn norms of behavior and patterns of communication that are often gender based, and sometimes gender biased. We also develop stereotypes about how and how much males and females—that is, boys and girls or women and men—should and do communicate. However, researchers have shown that many of these stereotypes actually turn out to be quite wrong.

Now, a common stereotype that many people hold is that women talk a lot, perhaps too much. And that they are always interrupting or trying to take "center stage" when someone else is talking. Actually, recent research on the influence of gender on communication has shown the exact opposite is true in many instances!

Researchers have found that men usually produce more talk than women. And men are more likely to interrupt another speaker than women are—particularly in public settings, such as business meetings. So although women are believed to talk more than men, study after study has shown that it is men who talk more at meetings, in mixed-group discussions, and in classrooms where girls or young women sit next to boys or young men. And this finding holds even for communicative interactions between very educated and successful professional men and women, such as professors, for example.

Deborah Tannen, in her book *You Just Don't Understand*, cites a study conducted by Barbara and Gene Eakins, who recorded and studied seven university faculty meetings. They found that, with one exception, male professors spoke more often and, without exception, for a longer period of time than the female professors did. The men took center stage and talked from 10.66 seconds to 17.07 seconds, while the women talked from 3 to 10 seconds, on the average. Tannen points out that the women's longest turns were still shorter than the men's shortest turns. Angela Simeone reported another example of this phenomenon in her book, *Academic Women*. She found that women professors talk at departmental meetings less often than their male colleagues do. When asked how often they spoke at departmental meetings, 46 percent of the American men professors reported that they spoke often at these meetings, but only 15 percent of the women professors reported that they spoke often at departmental meetings.

Well, perhaps it's our social concept of what is feminine and what is masculine that reinforces the stereotype that women talk more than men, and even causes these different patterns of communication. Maybe a woman is labeled talkative or is criticized for interrupting, if she does these things at all, because our culture—in fact, many cultures—teaches that women should be quiet if they want to be "feminine." Perhaps masculine culture encourages boys and men to dominate talk and to interrupt more often, and males who talk a lot and interrupt often are not criticized for doing so.

These differences in the patterns of communication and styles of communicating are studied by researchers who examine the effects of gender on communication. They study these effects in order to understand why misunderstandings occur between men and women in conversation. Often, it's because their styles and patterns of conversation are so different. It's important that we learn to recognize these differences so that we can learn to communicate better with people of the other gender. It's important to emphasize that these differences may be specific to North American culture. Gender can affect communication in even more and stronger ways in some other cultures. In Zulu culture, for example, a wife is forbidden to say any words that sound like the names of her father-in-law or brothers. This means that she must paraphrase and find other ways to say these things, and she is expected to do so.

So you see, cultural differences are not the only things that affect language and communication. Language is affected by gender as well. I'm sure you can think of many ways that gender affects communication between men and women in your own culture.

SECOND LISTENING Page 82

See First Listening, above.

THIRD LISTENING Page 82

Part 1

Lecturer: Now, a common stereotype that many people hold is that women talk a lot, perhaps too much. And that they are always interrupting or trying to take "center stage" when someone else is talking. Actually, recent research on the influence of gender on communication has shown the exact opposite is true in many instances!

Mentor

1. *Look at number one. Do you see how the information in* a *is very clear because spacing and symbols are used so effectively? When you look at* a, *the main idea jumps right out.*

   Now look at b. *Do you see the problem? You should not try to write full sentences in your notes. If your notes look like* b, *you need to learn to use abbreviations and symbols rather than full words and sentences.*

   What about c? *Although there is a contrast in this part of the lecture, it is not a contrast between men and women; it is a contrast between a stereotype and reality. That kind of gets lost in* c. *And there is only one contrast, so a chart isn't necessary. I used* a *in my notes.*

Part 2

Lecturer: Deborah Tannen, in her book *You Just Don't Understand*, cites a study conducted by Barbara and Gene Eakins, who recorded and studied seven university faculty meetings. They found that, with one exception, male professors spoke more often and, without exception, for a longer period of time than the female professors did. The men took center stage and talked from 10.66 seconds to 17.07 seconds, while the women talked from 3 to 10 seconds, on the average. Tannen points out that the women's longest turns were still shorter than the men's shortest turns. Angela Simeone reported another example of this phenomenon in her book, *Academic Women*. She found that women professors talk at departmental meetings less often than their male colleagues do. When asked how often they spoke at departmental meetings, 46 percent of the American men professors reported that they spoke often at these meetings, but only 15 percent of the women professors reported that they spoke often at departmental meetings.

Mentor

2. *Now look at the notes in number two. The information in* a *and* b *is similar, and they both use a chart, which was a good idea because this part of the lecture involved some contrasts; however, the charts are organized differently. Which presents the information more clearly?*

   Well, b *highlights the differences between the two research studies quite clearly. However, it doesn't highlight the differences between males and females as well as* a *does. And because showing the differences between male and female communication patterns was the main point, with the research studies illustrating that point,* a *works better than* b. *My notes are in* a.

Part 3

Lecturer: Well, perhaps it is our social concept of what is feminine and what is masculine that reinforces the stereotype that women talk more than men, and even causes these different patterns of communication. Maybe a woman is labeled talkative or is criticized for interrupting if she does these things at all, because our culture—in fact, many cultures—teaches that women should be quiet if they want to be "feminine." Perhaps masculine culture encourages boys and men to dominate talk and to interrupt more often, and males who talk a lot and interrupt often are not criticized for doing so.

Mentor

3. *Look at number three. The lecturer's main point here was to explain why people think that women talk more than men, when in fact the opposite is true.*

   Both a *and* b *contain the important information but* b *is clearer. The point that people think women talk more than men, when in fact the opposite is true, is a little complicated. More information, as in* b, *is needed.*

   In b, *a heading above the chart introduces the topic: cultural expectations. And the column headings specifically say these are* roles *that women and men are expected to play. The headings in* a *don't make that clear.*

   The use of so *in* b *makes the relationship between the ideas clearer than they are in* a. *The notes in* b *are mine.*

ACCURACY CHECK Page 83

1. How do children learn culturally appropriate patterns of communication?
2. According to Deborah Tannen, which of the following statements is true about American girls and boys?
3. What is one of the main differences between how boys and girls play?
4. What is one of the main differences between how boys and girls communicate?
5. Why do boys try to take center stage?
6. Which of the following is an example of a child practicing a gender role?
7. Which of the statements is an inaccurate stereotype about the differences between male and female communication?
8. The lecturer mentions Zulu culture as an example of what?

UNIT 5

Biology: From Genetics to Genetic Engineering

CHAPTER 9

The Origins of Genetics: Mendel and the Garden Pea Experiment

VOCABULARY PREVIEW Page 91

A

1. Genes determine how every living creature on earth appears, how it functions, how it reproduces, and generally, how it behaves.
2. Inherited traits, or characteristics, are determined by combinations of genes that are different for every human being.
3. The scientists who study how genes are inherited and passed from one generation to the next are called geneticists.
4. I want to acknowledge and briefly examine the work of a pioneer in biology, Gregor Mendel.
5. Mendel studied science at the University of Vienna, and there he learned how to use mathematics to try to explain natural phenomena.
6. When a variety of garden pea that had violet flowers was crossed with a variety that had white flowers, all the offspring surprisingly had only violet flowers.
7. Mendel applied his knowledge of mathematics and statistics to help him predict the results of the

crossbreeding of the white-flowering and violet-flowering plants.

8. The pea plants could be cultivated quickly, and with little effort.
9. We now know that genes are tiny biochemical structures inside each cell that determine eye color, blood type, height, and so on.
10. A person may have a genetic tendency toward being overweight, but the person's actual weight will depend on a number of environmental factors.

NOTETAKING PREPARATION Page 92

B

1. These genes are passed down from one generation to the next, or inherited. You may, for example, have inherited the color of your hair from your mother.
2. Many of your individual traits resemble those of your parents—including the color and shape of your eyes, the texture of your hair, and even your height and weight.
3. Humans have always been interested in learning how to improve the breeding of animals to make them more valuable and useful. In the case of racehorses, for example, owners want to breed strong, beautiful, and fast horses that can run faster than their competitors' horses can run.
4. The garden pea plant has many traits that have two clearly different forms that are easy to tell apart, such as color—the color of a pea flower is either violet or white.
5. A person may have a genetic tendency toward being overweight, but the person's actual weight will also be influenced by a number of environmental factors, such as how much and what kinds of food the person eats, and how much exercise the person gets.

FIRST LISTENING Page 93

Lecturer: I'd like to begin today's lecture by asking a few simple questions. Why do people look different from cats, from horses, and from birds? Why do people look different from each other? Why do you look different from your sister or brother? The answer to all these questions lies in the genes of people and animals. Your genes provide biological instructions that control how you look, how you function, and even, partly, how you behave. Genes determine how every living creature on earth appears, functions, reproduces, and generally, behaves.

Now, genes are found inside the cells of the body. They're made up of deoxyribonucleic acid, or as we always call it, DNA. DNA contains instructions for what each of the genes is supposed to do. These genes are passed down from one generation to the next, or inherited. You may, for example, have inherited the color of your hair from your mother, or the ability to roll your tongue from your father. Or maybe you inherited some other interesting trait you may or may not be grateful for from your great, great, great grandfather or grandmother. Who knows? Inherited traits, or characteristics, are determined by combinations of genes that are different for every human being.

Now, although each individual is unique, it's interesting to note that most genes are common to every person on earth. In fact, humans share many of the same genes with other kinds, or species, of animals, from the simple, little fruit fly to our close cousins, the apes. In fact, and this might surprise you—humans and the small African ape called the bonobo, share about 97 percent of the same genes. I don't know whether that's good news or not for us—or for the bonobos.

The study of genes is a branch of the field of biology called genetics, and the scientists who study how genes are inherited and passed from one generation to the next are called geneticists. The field of genetics actually dates back to the mid-1800s, but most of what we know today about genes—and also about genetic disorders—has been learned in only the last few decades.

But I, I don't want to jump ahead to what's going on in modern genetics before we acknowledge, and briefly examine, the work of a pioneer in biology, Gregor Mendel. Mendel lived from 1822 to 1884. He carried out some of the earliest experiments in genetics by studying the simple pea plant.

Now, between 1856 and 1863, Mendel grew more than 28,000 pea plants, and he kept very careful records on these plants. From these records, he saw clearly that there was a predictable pattern by which plant traits or characteristics were passed from one generation of pea plant to the next—a pattern that had never been reported before. Mendel explained the patterns in principles, or laws. Today these principles are known as the Mendelian Laws of Heredity.

Because we're talking about Gregor Mendel, let me take a moment to tell you something interesting about him that might help you see the real man. Now, in 1843, Mendel joined an order of monks that had strong interests in science and culture, and he became a teacher. In 1851, he was sent to the University of Vienna to study mathematics and experimental biology—the two subjects that were to make him so famous throughout the world. After two years of study he left the University of Vienna to return to the monastery and to teaching. Mendel was extremely nervous and anxious about taking exams. It seems that this extreme nervousness about taking examinations kept him from taking the exam to be certified to continue teaching. Instead, when he returned to his monastery, Mendel began conducting his research and become one of the most famous scientists of all time.

All right, uh, let's see, where was I? Oh, yes. I was talking about genes and the passing of certain traits and characteristics from one generation to another. Many of your individual traits resemble those of your parents—including the color and shape of your eyes, the texture of your hair, and even your height and weight. Your parents have passed traits on to you, and this passing of traits from parent to offspring, as we know, is called "heredity."

From the earliest times, people have been interested in studying and understanding how heredity works. People have wanted to learn how they could alter crop plants, like corn, to give the corn traits that would make the corn crop larger and better tasting. And today farmers can do that. Humans have also always been interested in learning how to improve the breeding of animals to make them more valuable and useful. Um, let's see. In the case of racehorses, for example, owners want to breed strong, beautiful, and fast horses that can run faster than their competitors' horses. A famous racehorse, Seabiscuit, was the grandson of a champion racehorse named Man of War. Undoubtedly, Man of War passed on traits of strength and speed that helped his grandson Seabiscuit race faster than so many other horses, even though Seabiscuit was a small horse, compared to the larger horses he raced against.

OK. Well, to continue. Before DNA was discovered—that is, when Gregor Mendel began his experiments—heredity was one of the greatest mysteries of science. Now, as I mentioned earlier, Mendel studied science at the University of Vienna, and there he learned how to use mathematics to try to explain natural phenomena.

While in Vienna, Mendel studied the work of Thomas Knight, another early pioneer in the study of heredity and genetics. Knight had crossed a variety of garden pea that had violet flowers with a variety that had white flowers. To his surprise, he found that all of the offspring had only violet flowers. However, when two of the violet-flowered offspring were crossed, *their* offspring produced both violet and white flowers. The white-color trait had reappeared in the second generation of the plant. Knight was puzzled by this reappearance of the white flowers in the second generation, and he was unable to explain why this happened.

Mendel decided to repeat Knight's work on the garden pea plant—which is called *Pisum sativum* in Latin. But Mendel decided to apply his knowledge of mathematics and statistics to help him predict the results of the crossbreeding of the white-flowering and violet-flowering plants. OK. Now, you might ask why Mendel used a plant, rather than an animal, to study the puzzle of heredity, and why he used the simple garden pea, rather than a rose or some other flowering plant. Well, Mendel had a number of good reasons for choosing to study the pea plant. For one thing, this plant was readily available and plentiful where he lived in Austria. Second, the peas could be cultivated quickly, and with little effort. And most important—from a mathematician's perspective—the garden pea plant produced a large number of baby pea plants, or offspring.

Actually, it seems that the garden pea was a very good subject for studying heredity for several other reasons as well. The garden pea plant has many traits that have two clearly different forms that are easy to tell apart, such as color—the color of a pea flower is either violet or white. There is no intermediate color. Next, the mating of the garden-pea flowers can be easily manipulated, so Mendel was able to control the mating of the plant easily and then observe the offspring plants that resulted from the mating. As I mentioned at the beginning of the lecture, Mendel grew more than 28,000 plants, and recorded the many offspring of these plants. And he did all this counting and record keeping long before computers were available for record keeping and statistical analyses. Pretty impressive!

We're still benefiting today from the early research done by Gregor Mendel. As a result of his research, today we understand much more about genetics and heredity, though there is still so much more to be learned.

We now know that genes are tiny biochemical structures inside each cell. They determine particular hereditary traits, such as eye color, blood type, height, and so on. But we must remember that the gene gives only the potential for the development of a particular trait. How this potential is realized, or achieved, depends partly on the interaction of the gene with other genes. And it depends partly on the environment. For example, a person may have a genetic tendency to be overweight, but the person's actual weight will also be influenced by a number of environmental factors, such as how much and what kinds of food the person eats, and how much exercise the person gets. Yes, we are what we eat, and thanks to the fact that our ancestors ate—we are! And on that note, my inherited hunger trait is telling me that it's almost time for lunch, so we'll stop there.

SECOND LISTENING Page 95

See First Listening, above.

THIRD LISTENING Page 95

Part 1

Lecturer: Now, genes are found inside the cells of the body. They're made up of deoxyribonucleic acid, or as we always call it, DNA. DNA contains instructions for what each of the genes is supposed to do. These genes are passed down from one generation to the next, or inherited. You may, for example, have inherited the color of your hair from your mother, or the ability to roll your tongue from your father. Or maybe you inherited some other interesting trait you may or may not be grateful for from your great, great, great grandfather or grandmother. Who knows? Inherited traits, or characteristics, are determined by combinations of genes that are different for every human being.

Although each individual is unique, it's interesting to note that most genes are common to every person on earth. In fact, humans share many of the same genes with other kinds, or species, of animals, from the simple, little fruit fly to our close cousins, the apes. In fact, and this might surprise you—humans and the small African ape called the bonobo, share about 97 percent of the same genes. I don't know whether that's good news or not for us—or for the bonobos.

Mentor

1. *Look at number one. Which notes are similar to your notes? You can probably guess that the notes in* a *are better, but let's consider why.*

   First, a *uses indentation to show how the information relates to genes. Notice that the word* genes *does not need to be written again, as it does in* b.

   Notetaker a *saves time by writing the common abbreviation "DNA," but* b *tried to spell out the full name, which wasn't necessary. Also,* a *recorded "body cells," which means the same thing as "cells of our body" but takes less time to write.*

   Finally, b *includes details that are not needed. If you know the meaning of "inherited traits," you do not need to include "from your grandmother or grandfather."*

   The notes in a *are mine.*

Part 2

Lecturer: Because we're talking about Gregor Mendel, let me take a moment to tell you something interesting about him that might help you see the real man. Now, in 1843, Mendel joined an order of monks that had strong interests in science and culture, and he became a teacher. In 1851, he was sent to the University of Vienna to study mathematics and experimental biology—the two subjects that were to make him so famous throughout the world. After two years of study he left the University of Vienna to return to the monastery and to teaching. Mendel was extremely nervous and anxious about taking exams. It seems that this extreme nervousness about taking examinations kept him from taking the exam to be certified to continue teaching. Instead, when he returned to his monastery Mendel began conducting his research and become one of the most famous scientists of all time.

Mentor

2. *Look at number two. How do your notes compare with the three sets of notes that you see?*

   It might look like notetaker c *fell asleep. But this student decided* not *to take notes. The lecturer used the phrase "let me take a moment." This usually signals a digression—information that is not important to the topic, and therefore it probably isn't necessary to take notes. The lecturer also said, "that might help you see the real man," another clue that the information that follows will not be related to genetics.*

   The notes in b *were mine. I began recording some biographical information about Mendel, just in case it might be helpful later on, but then I stopped and listened to the story. Notetaker* a *could have relaxed and done the same thing.*

Part 3

Lecturer: While in Vienna, Mendel studied the work of Thomas Knight, another early pioneer in the study of heredity and genetics. Knight had crossed a variety of the garden pea that had violet flowers with a variety that had white flowers. To his surprise, he found that all of the offspring had only violet flowers. However, when two of the violet-flowered offspring were crossed, *their* offspring produced both violet and white flowers. The white-color trait had reappeared in the second generation of the plant. Knight was puzzled by this reappearance of the white flowers in the second generation, and he was unable to explain why this happened.

Mentor

3. *Look at number three. These notes record Thomas Knight's early experiments with pea plants. Which notes are similar to yours?*

   I took the notes in b. *As you see, I decided to use pictures, arrows, and spatial relations to show what happened when Knight crossed plants with violet and white flowers over three generations.*

   Both a *and* b *use an* X *to show crossing, or breeding, and both use an exclamation point to show an unexpected result. The notes in* a *are certainly fine, and not everyone is comfortable drawing pictures as in* b.

   The notes in b *have some advantages. They clearly show the different generations. In* a *the term* offspring *is used for two different generations. That could be confusing when the student reviews these notes later.*

ACCURACY CHECK Page 96

1. What do genes determine?
2. How much difference is there in the genes of different people?
3. How much do bonobo genes differ from human genes?
4. How old is the field of genetics?
5. What did Gregor Mendel study at the University of Vienna?
6. What did Mendel learn about pea plants from his research?

7. What is one reason why nonscientists have long been interested in understanding heredity?
8. Name a human trait that is completely determined by heredity.

CHAPTER 10

Genetic Engineering: Playing Roulette with Mother Nature's Designs?

VOCABULARY PREVIEW Page 100

A

1. I'll be touching on some of the important advances that have been made in recent years using genetic engineering, and also some of the controversies that have arisen.
2. The new DNA causes the organism to function in a different way, and this function or trait can then be inherited by succeeding generations.
3. One way to increase productivity is to make plants resistant to disease so that more of the crop survives and is harvested.
4. Transgenic Bt crops produce enough toxin to actually kill the harmful insect, so farmers don't need to spray their crops with insecticides.
5. If it is approved by the FDA—that's the U.S. government agency that regulates food—the genetically modified salmon would be the first genetically altered animal to be approved for human consumption in the United States.
6. The genetically altered fish has never been eaten before, and it could cause dangerous allergies, especially because seafood tends to be quite allergenic.
7. Environmentalists are concerned that the fish will escape and breed with the wild salmon population, which is already endangered.
8. The FDA granted marketing approval for transgenic goat antithrombin, the first drug to be produced in genetically modified livestock.
9. Ethicists have questions about gene therapy.
10. How long will it be before we're screening—and maybe selecting—human embryos for characteristics such as physical strength?

NOTETAKING PREPARATION Page 101

B

1. We call the modified organism "transgenic" because it contains genes that were transferred from a different organism.
2. One way is to engineer them for drought resistance—so that they can thrive in areas where there is limited water.
3. Or it can be done in germ line cells, where the effect can be passed down to that person's offspring.
4. To create more of the drug, you use cloning technology to reproduce the plant or animal.
5. It produces milk containing antithrombin, a protein that is very important in preventing the formation of blood clots.

FIRST LISTENING Page 102

Lecturer: All right, in our last session together I talked about two major issues in biology. One of the major issues I talked about was the importance of Mendel's experiments on the garden pea plant, and his findings about how certain traits are passed from one generation to the next. The other major issue I talked about was the role heredity and genetics play in who we are, what we look like, and to some extent, how we behave.

Today, I'll be talking about genetic engineering. I'll go over what genetic engineering is, and then I'll be touching on some of the important advances that have been made in recent years using genetic engineering. And I'll also discuss some controversies that have arisen, uh, specific concerns that some people have about genetic engineering. Some of these concerns are practical and others are ethical. I'll be giving some examples of genetic engineering projects in the field of agriculture, and also in the field of medicine.

All right, what do we mean by "genetically modified"—GM—or "genetically engineered"? A genetically engineered, or genetically modified organism—or a GMO, as they are sometimes called—is an organism whose genetic material has been altered by the introduction of DNA from a different source. This new DNA causes the organism to function in a different way, and this function or trait can then be inherited by succeeding generations, whether it's a plant or an animal. The new trait can then be passed on. We call the modified organism "transgenic" because it contains *genes* that were *transferred* from a different organism.

Now, what kinds of desired modifications could we be talking about here? Well, as I said earlier, one area where this technology is very widely used is in the field of agriculture, to improve either livestock or crops, such as corn and wheat.

So let's start off with the field of agriculture. We can see the evidence of genetic engineering of crops sitting right on the supermarket shelves, probably in that box of corn flakes you bought at the supermarket recently. I'm going to give you some statistics that may surprise you: An estimated 85 percent of the corn grown in the United States is genetically modified; 91 percent of soybeans are genetically modified; 88 percent of cotton. And nearly 70 percent of processed foods—that includes soft drinks, soup, crackers—are genetically modified. Now, let me add that outside the United States those percentages are lower and there has been greater resistance to GMOs. But at least in the United States, use of GMOs is widespread. Is this something to be concerned about?

All right, let's consider why we would want to modify foods, and in what way. We'll talk about the specific goals of genetic engineering in agriculture, how the creation of GMOs has achieved or is trying to achieve these goals, and what concerns have arisen as a result.

The primary goal is to increase food production worldwide. The area of our planet that is currently used for agricultural production is decreasing every year, and meanwhile the world population is increasing. So, there is an ongoing need for greater productivity in agriculture, if we are going to feed the world, now and in the future. How, specifically, do you increase productivity? Well, one way is to make plants disease and insect resistant, so that more of the crop survives and is harvested. Corn, peanuts, and potatoes have all been transgenically modified to be resistant to harmful insects, by introduction of a gene that produces a toxin called *Bacillus thuringiensis*, or Bt. When an insect eats Bt corn or Bt peanuts, the toxin kills the insect. Transgenic Bt crops produce enough toxin to actually kill the harmful insect, so farmers don't need to spray their crops with insecticides, which are bad because they also kill the good insects. And the result is healthier and bigger crops. So, is there a downside to Bt crops? Well, yes. The fact is that in nature, when an organism is exposed to a toxin, over time it develops a resistance to the toxin—in other words, it takes more toxin to kill it. And already we see that with Bt cotton crops in some parts of India, where there is a worm that is now resistant to Bt. So that is a challenge for genetic engineers.

OK, what are some other ways to modify crops to increase production? One is to engineer them for drought resistance so that they can thrive in areas where there is limited water. Also, crops have been genetically engineered to ripen more slowly so that they can be shipped great distances without spoiling.

Another way to increase global food production is to engineer crops or animals to mature more quickly. We see an example of this in aquaculture, which is the most rapidly growing area of agriculture today. Salmon farming accounts for a large part of aquaculture. By 2007, nearly 70 percent of the world's salmon was raised on fish farms. Recently, a biotech company has created a transgenic salmon by introducing a growth hormone from a different kind of salmon, and the resulting fish reaches adult size twice as fast. If it is approved by the FDA—that's the U.S. government agency that regulates food—the GM salmon would be the first genetically altered *animal* to be approved for human consumption in the United States. Now, as I have said, in the United States the public has become more or less accepting of GM crops—corn, wheat, tomatoes, soybeans. But what about animals? What about fish?

The fact is that the GM salmon—and some people call it a "Frankenfish," a reference to that famous story about the monster—the fish has met with enormous resistance from the American public. Why? Critics have two main concerns. First, its safety for human consumption: The genetically altered fish has never been eaten before and it could cause dangerous allergies, especially because seafood tends to be quite allergenic. And second, the potential environmental impact: Environmentalists are concerned that the fish will escape and breed with the wild salmon population, which is already endangered. Or the genetically modified "super salmon" could simply wipe out the *wild* salmon's food supply.

So, yes, GMOs have contributed to increases in global food production; but controversies and practical concerns remain.

OK. Now let's turn to genetic engineering in medicine. The first area I'll mention is the production of pharmaceuticals—drugs—by genetic engineering. This is sometimes referred to as "pharming" spelled with a *P-H* instead of an *F*. As you can guess, it refers to agricultural production, or farming, of pharmaceuticals, in which a gene that produces a useful drug is inserted into the cells of a host animal or plant. The host then begins to produce the drug—for example, insulin. This is more economical than having to produce it in a laboratory. And then to create more of the drug, you use cloning technology to reproduce the plant or animal. Some examples are safflower, a plant that produces an oil used in cooking. A GM version of safflower that produces insulin has been developed. Another example is a transgenic goat that produces milk containing antithrombin, a protein that is very important in preventing the formation of blood clots. In 2009 the FDA granted marketing approval for transgenic goat antithrombin, the first drug to be produced in genetically modified livestock.

OK. Another area where genetic engineering is used is in the creation of animal models of human diseases. Genetically modified mice are the most commonly used. One common practice is to remove a gene from a mouse, creating what is called a "knockout mouse." Knocking out the activity of a gene provides information about what that gene normally does. It turns out that humans and mice share many genes, so observing the characteristics of knockout mice gives researchers information that can be used to better understand how a similar gene may cause or contribute to disease in humans.

Knockout mice have been used to research many diseases and conditions, including, cancers, uh, obesity, heart disease, diabetes, arthritis, anxiety, aging, and Parkinson's disease.

Finally, gene therapy, which is the genetic engineering of humans by replacing defective human genes with functional copies. This can be done in somatic cells, that is, where the effect is on the body of only a particular individual, or in germ line cells, where the effect can be passed down to that person's offspring. Gene therapy has been used to treat patients suffering from immune deficiencies and research on some other genetic disorders is ongoing. However, success has been limited and there have been a few deaths associated with gene therapy.

Also, ethicists have questions about gene therapy. Should this technology be used only for treatment of disease? If a person wants to use it to improve their physical appearance, or live longer, should they be able to? And to be honest, questions like this are overly simplistic because most human traits are caused by multiple genes in complex combinations that we do not yet understand. So we might say that gene therapy raises practical as well as ethical concerns.

However, we will probably have to face questions like this in the future: Should we be able to change ourselves through genetic engineering? Another even more controversial question: Should a couple expecting a baby be able to make sure, through genetic screening, that the child they're expecting will not be born with some hereditary disorder, such as very poor eyesight, or mental depression, or even a tendency to be overweight? With the knowledge we have of human genetics, and with the techniques we have for both newborn and prenatal screening, how long will it be before we're screening—and maybe selecting—human embryos for characteristics such as physical strength, or other qualities such as eye color, hair color . . . you name it?

OK. So we've looked at how far we have come in understanding and manipulating genetics. But there are still a great many unknowns concerning the environmental and human consequences of our actions. Do we really know what we're doing, or are we "playing roulette with Mother Nature?"

Whatever you may think about the ethics of the genetic engineering of humans or animals, today biologists are using genetic engineering for two main purposes: (1) in agriculture, to address the global need for food; and (2) in medicine, to make newer and, they hope, better drugs and to cure disease.

OK. Well, that is a lot to think about.

SECOND LISTENING Page 104

See First Listening, above.

THIRD LISTENING Page 104

Part 1

Lecturer: Today, I'll be talking about genetic engineering. I'll go over what genetic engineering is, and then I'll be touching on some of the important advances that have been made in recent years using genetic engineering. And I'll also discuss some controversies that have arisen, uh, specific concerns that some people have about genetic engineering. Some of these concerns are practical and others are ethical. I'll be giving some examples of genetic engineering projects in the field of agriculture, and also in the field of medicine.

Mentor

1. *Look at number one. Which notes are most similar to yours? Circle the letter.*

   If your notes look like b, *you did a great job of recording the preview of the lecture and using outline form to show what it seems will be the structure and order. However, in giving a preview, a lecturer does not always list everything in chronological order. The outline in* b *shows the examples of genetic engineering projects in agriculture and medicine as coming at the end of the lecture. In fact, that was not the case, and it may be confusing when the lecturer doesn't follow the outline in* b.

   I took the notes in a. *I noticed that the lecturer's comment "I'll be giving examples of projects" was a simple statement, not introduced by "then" or "next," so I guessed that the examples from agriculture and medicine might not come at the end, though I wasn't sure exactly where they would be. Notice where I put this information in my notes. Also, I didn't know the word* controversies, *so I wrote the first letters with a line and question mark. When the lecturer then gave an explanation, I wrote that on the line and crossed out those first letters and question mark.*

Part 2

Lecturer: All right, let's consider why we would want to modify foods, and in what way. We'll talk about the specific goals of genetic engineering in agriculture, how the creation of GMOs has achieved or is trying to achieve these goals, and what concerns have arisen as a result.

The primary goal is to increase food production worldwide. The area of our planet that is currently used for agricultural production is decreasing every year, and meanwhile the world population is increasing. So there is an ongoing need for greater productivity in agriculture, if we are going to feed the world, now and in the future. How, specifically, do you increase productivity? Well, one way is to make plants disease and insect resistant, so that more of the crop survives and is harvested. Corn, peanuts, and potatoes have all been transgenically modified to be resistant to harmful insects, by introduction of a gene that produces a toxin called *Bacillus thuringiensis*, or Bt. When an insect eats Bt corn or Bt peanuts, the toxin kills the insect. Transgenic Bt crops produce enough toxin to actually kill the harmful insect, so farmers don't need to spray their crops with insecticides, which are bad because they also kill the good insects. And the result is healthier and bigger crops. So, is there a downside to Bt crops? Well, yes. The fact is that in nature, when an organism is exposed to a toxin, over time it develops a resistance to the toxin—in other words, it takes more toxin to kill it. And already we see that with Bt cotton crops in some parts of India, where there is a worm that is now resistant to Bt. So that is a challenge for genetic engineers.

Mentor

2. *Look at number two. Which notes are more similar to yours?*

Notice that in a Bacillus thuringiensis *isn't spelled out; instead the abbreviation* Bt *is used.* A *uses symbols more than* b *does.*

Also, you probably noticed that this lecturer likes to preview what will be said. When this happens at the beginning, it is useful to note down the overall structure as it is previewed. But as the lecture goes into more detail, it does not make sense to take notes. For example, when the lecturer says "we will talk about," listen, and wait until the lecturer actually talks about it. Which notes show the writer just listened during this minipreview and which show the writer took notes? [pause] Yes, a *just listened. The notes in* a *are mine.*

Part 3

Lecturer: Now let's turn to genetic engineering in medicine. The first area I'll mention is the production of pharmaceuticals—drugs—by genetic engineering. This is sometimes referred to as "pharming" spelled with a *P-H* instead of an *F*. As you can guess, it refers to agricultural production, or farming, of pharmaceuticals, in which a gene that produces a useful drug is inserted into the cells of a host animal or plant. The host then begins to produce the drug—for example, insulin. This is more economical than having to produce it in a laboratory. And then to create more of the drug, you use cloning technology to reproduce the plant or animal. Some examples are safflower, a plant that produces an oil used in cooking. A GM version of safflower that produces insulin has been developed. Another example is a transgenic goat that produces milk containing antithrombin, a protein that is very important in preventing the formation of blood clots.

Mentor

3. *Look at number three. Which notes are most like yours?*

Compare how a *and* b *record the process of creating a transgenic plant or animal. Which do you think is clearer? I took the notes in* b. *I think the numbered steps are easier to follow than the notes in* a.

In a *the notetaker tried to spell* pharmaceuticals. *You don't need to do this because the lecturer gives a familiar synonym:* drugs. *You can look up how to spell* pharmaceutical *later. The lecturer also explains the word* pharming*—spelled with P-H. You don't need to write a definition of* pharming. *The spelling will help you remember that is a combination of* farming *and the* p-h *word that means "drugs."*

Notice that a *has a longer abbreviation than* b *for "genetic engineering." I used the letters GE. At this point in the lecture you do not need to write anything longer than GE for genetic engineering; you are not likely to forget what it stands for.*

The notes in a *include a definition of* antithrombin. *In* b, *I wrote as much of the word as I could and will look it up later to find out what it means.*

Finally, in this part of the lecture the verb produce *is used many times. Notice that* a *uses the synonym* make, *which is short and easy to abbreviate. But other abbreviations in* a *could be confusing later, such as* m-r *for* more. *If* a *always uses* m-r *for* more, *that is absolutely fine. The important thing to remember is to use symbols and abbreviations in a consistent way.*

ACCURACY CHECK Page 105

1. What does a transgenic plant or animal have that makes it different?
2. The lecture discusses advances in two fields. Which is *not* included?
3. What is the main goal of genetic engineering in agriculture?
4. Give an example of genetically modified livestock mentioned in the lecture.
5. What disadvantage of transgenic Bt crops is mentioned in the lecture?
6. Why is genetically modified salmon controversial?
7. What has gene therapy been used to treat?
8. Which of the following uses of human genetic engineering is *least* controversial?

APPENDIX B

Videoscripts

UNIT 1 VIDEO

The Gift of Traveling

Our kids have traveled to every continent except Antarctica. More importantly, when we travel they have lived in communities. We never stayed in hotels. And so they were always in little communities where they were hanging out with kids. And sometimes they had language in common, and many times they did not. And they've learned how to have fun the way those kids had fun.

And they're very confident travelers. Our daughter—you know, she's 18 now and she has no problem hopping on a plane and going overseas. And it is not a stressful thing for her. She really is excited about it and remembers all of our trips with, you know, enthusiasm and great memories. So, and I think they also—our kids—I think our kids also understand that people all over the world are different, that you don't assume that they are going to be the same as we are. But that if you go into each culture open and look people in the eye and observe and listen, you're going to make connections that are well beyond what most travelers get to see. And I think what I've learned from my kids is how delightful flexibility is and how naturally flexible most kids are, as long as they've got the basics. You know, food and sleep and a little something to keep them entertained. They pretty much can set up camp anywhere.

Almost everything's been photographed. And so the real challenge for a photographer is to bring her or his own unique vision to that subject matter. And in the case of the work that I do on assignment, it's primarily telling a story that is compelling enough—where you know the photograph is compelling enough to get people interested in reading the captions or what's going on. And hopefully that will lead them into a more in-depth written piece.

What traveling has taught me is that once, you know, step into another culture and you allow yourself to really immerse yourself in another culture and be available to them, communication happens very quickly. And it doesn't require perfect language skills. It doesn't require introductions. It's really something that happens when you are your honest self, when you recognize that you are a guest in another culture and that you really need to listen to people on a different level and abide by their way of doing things. That's the best part of travel for me. In fact, it's kind of spoiled regular travel for me because the camera has always given me an opportunity to walk up to people and spend time with them and even go home with them.

I think one of the most inspirational parts about photography is that you're never done. You're always growing, and when you travel you're always learning. So to have a career where I get to be creative, I'm immersed in really interesting situations, and I continue to grow artistically. What's better than that?

UNIT 2 VIDEO

Palenque

George Stuart: Hello there. It's good to be back. As you can see from this wonderful photograph, the site itself—Palenque—sits on a kind of a shelf. The place sits in Chiapas, down here in the Maya area. And there's Palenque right there. Archeology came to Palenque in 1934. When Mexico formed its National Institute of Anthropology and History, they sent Miguel Angel Fernandez there to start digging the palace.

When they finished the palace, they started looking over the temple and the inscriptions. This was how it was in 1942, and 1948, when Alberto Ruiz was hired to start. And he walked in the temple up there and he noticed something. And that is, that the floor of the temple was made out of big, stone slabs with holes in them. So Alberto had the workers pull up the stone. And underneath the stone there were two steps leading down. He didn't know whether it went down four more feet and stopped, or whether there were three steps. At the end of the summer of '48, he'd gone down 23 steps.

Finally, in June of 1952, he walked into this empty room at the bottom, and there was nothing there. And Juan Chablé, who was one of the masons, the head mason, said, "Don Alberto, there's a funny-looking, little triangular stone over there against the wall, if we could move that, I'll bet you there's something behind it." So they moved the triangular stone aside, and there was a room—a room with a stone in it. He thought it was an altar, a table. He didn't know what it was; nobody had ever found anything like that. And then he came back and Juan Chablé, the mason, said, "Hey, Don Alberto, why don't you drill a hole in the side of this thing and see if it's hollow?" He did, and it was. We went into town and got 15 automobile jacks and pulled the thing up, and there was a body inside. And so what I'm going to do is let David take the story here for a while and talk about the man in the tomb.

David Stuart: Okay, we're going to shift gears a little bit and look at a lot of detail at what turned out to be, I guess, the American equivalent—if there is one—to King Tut's tomb. His full name was K'inich Janaab' Pakal, and he was the greatest king of Palenque, one of the greatest of all Maya kings. Now, Pakal was born in the year 603 AD. We know from the inscriptions. He came to power in 615. So he was 12 years old when he became king. This is an early photograph of Pakal himself, in his tomb, after the inner slab was lifted. He was covered in jade, as a good Maya king would be. A jade collar, jade bracelets, and an extraordinary mask as well.

Here is Pakal. What you're seeing here, of course, is some of the jade and the mask. Unbelievable.

Years and years after he's dead, Pakal is still at the center of everything. And this is why I think Palenque—what we, most of what we see of Palenque in that central area—is Pakal City. It's just an incredible place to be, and it will always have that aura about it, I hope.

UNIT 3 VIDEO

An Actor and a Travel Writer

Interviewer: How did acting enter your life? How did you become an actor? How did you get started?

McCarthy: Good grief. I had just gotten cut from the high school basketball team and I was moping around the house, and my mother said, "Why don't you go try out for the play, dear?" I'm like, "I don't want to be in a play." And so I did, and that experience, I have to say, changed my life. My life suddenly made sense to me in a way it hadn't before. I felt like I belonged in a way I'd never experienced before. I felt powerful, seen, and I wanted to be seen. Whereas opposed to before that I'd been very reticent and shy. And I knew it was important because I told no one. I told . . . I didn't tell anyone how important . . . , "Yea, yea, it was good. I liked it, yea. When's the next one?" And so then I went to college for acting, and I took it more seriously, and it took me more seriously. And after two years of college, I was kicked out of college and got a job as an actor. And then it sort of happened very quickly for me. So that's how it began.

Interviewer: And then one role led to another led to another?

McCarthy: Well, then I didn't work for a year, and then I got a job as the Burger King boy in a commercial. No, I was the Pepsi boy in the Burger King commercial. And so that supported me for a few years, that commercial. And then I got another job. And then suddenly I got jobs very quickly, and I was suddenly a 22-year-old star.

Interviewer: So how did travel writing enter this equation?

McCarthy: It entered because at a certain point in my life, when I was about 30, I looked up and said, "Huh?" So I started reading a lot of travel literature, and I thought it was a very interesting genre, you know. So, I just started traveling. I just started buying tickets to places, you know buy a ticket into Cape Town and out of Dar es Salaam two months later. And the rest I'd just fill in. Or I'd go to Southeast Asia and just go for a while. And so every year I would, you know, take a couple months and do that. And I started just sort of writing little things. I wasn't keeping a journal in any way, but I would write little scenes of encounters I had with people. Just for myself, I'd write just sort of a scene . . . because that's what I knew how to do, was be in scenes. So I'd write the scene between me and the kid who picked me up, you know, on the moped in Hanoi and took me around for the day. And I would write that scene. I did nothing with them. I sat them in a drawer.

Interviewer: When you look at your life do you feel like you're more an actor, or a travel writer?

McCarthy: I'm just a guy, I don't know, I don't, I don't think of it that way. My life's sort of transitioning, you know. I'll always be the guy who was in *Pretty in Pink*, you know? I mean so that's okay, you know. Hopefully I'll be in some other things, too, you know, but that's certainly part of who I am. You know I wouldn't be here, sitting here, if I wasn't in those movies. You know what I mean? I may be a travel writer . . . you wouldn't be talking to just some travel writer. You know what I mean? So it's given me opportunities and opened doors for me and, you know, so it's just part of my story.

Interviewer: Well, thank you, Andrew, for a really, really delightful evening. Thank you very much.

UNIT 4 VIDEO

Digital Nomad

So, on New Year's Day, I head out from this very building, National Geographic Headquarters. It was symbolic. I wanted to show that I was just like these explorers who were sent out by the *Geographic* to go explore the world. And I was going to start from this very point on earth, and I was going to go to the bottom of the world. And I just got to the bus station on the S2 bus, which runs just outside Sixteenth Street, and I paid my fare, which was $1.35, and I got on the bus and took off. And here I am sending my first Tweet, a real-time narrative.

Now, this was an experiment for me, because all of the original explorers would go and they would keep a journal, and they would write about their trip, and then they would come home and actually write a book and publish. And this was a past tense kind of memoir about their journey. Well, I wanted to do this same thing, but I wanted to do it in real time. I just wanted to write the story as it was happening.

And I learned something, because I sent over 5,000 Tweets when I traveled from Washington, D.C., to Antarctica. And I learned that there was a more effective way to write on Twitter and a less effective. And for those who don't know Twitter, you know it's a way to share by text message. You're limited to 140 characters so you have to keep it really short. But you can say so much if you do it right. Now, I didn't start out as a pro. I'm still not a pro, but I'm learning, and I learned a lot from poets. This is one of my favorite poems by Jack Kerouac. It's from his American haiku, written in 1959: "Nightfall, boy smashing dandelions with a stick." Now, this follows an ancient Japanese form of poetry. But it's very short and it has all the great ingredients of a Tweet, of storytelling. He has set the stage. He's given you time. He's given you place. He's given you color. He's given you a character. And he's given you action. And you need all of these things when you're writing Twitter.

I've Tweeted from hot-air balloons. I've Tweeted from birchbark canoes. I've Tweeted above Niagara Falls in a helicopter. I've Tweeted from camelbacks. And I've Tweeted—not underwater, that doesn't work yet, but almost. I Tweeted in real time while flying a plane, in French.

Now I just want to leave with a couple of little tips for all of you digital nomads out there, things that I've learned that have helped me. One, besides being there, which is very important, always be there. Never let the experience of, you know, never let sharing the experience eclipse having the experience. And that's very possible. You can walk into any coffee shop here and you're going to see a million people with their phones, looking down like this. And it's very hard to experience the world around you when you're doing this.

This is in Botswana, in the Okavango Delta, beautiful place surrounded by wildlife, and I was with two journalists from New York. And we're out there, surrounded by lions, and all they cared about was that there was no reception on their phone. And there was one spot by the river near the Namibian border where there was a wildebeest carcass. And they always wanted to drive by the carcass, because the carcass, for whatever reason, had coverage. So they could always download their e-mail and their Tweets whenever we got by the carcass. So they were always like, "Let's go to the carcass, let's go to the carcass." And they were so obsessed with that, they missed out everything else that we were around. And if you're so obsessed with kind of sharing the experience, you miss the things that are around you.

There's one fourth tip that I have and I'll close with this. And that is, you have to unplug periodically. And if you don't, you just become crazed because the human mind works very different than our digital technology. Our minds are fascinating. We have subconsciouses that are always working. We take much better pictures than cameras do. We feel a place. We have these emotions. But if we don't shut off, we're not able to process that and share it. So, I'll just leave with that. You should unplug. You will sleep much better if you do. And I want to thank all of you for coming tonight and listening to my stories. Really grateful.

UNIT 5 VIDEO

The Human Journey

We have a huge amount of diversity as a species. We travel the world, walk down the street in a major city like Washington or New York, and we see people who seem to be so different from each other and from ourselves. We as population geneticists are trying to address the question of, well, you know, what is it that led to us being so successful and how do we explain these patterns of diversity that we see when we look around the world? Are we in fact all related to each other, and if so, how closely? And the other question is one of journey. If we do spring from a common source, as a species, how do we come to occupy every corner of the globe, in the process, generating these patterns of diversity that we see today in all seven billion of us and growing?

Well, historically, these questions have been approached through the study of stones and bones, often the field of paleoanthropology, and of course archaeology, its sister science—going out and digging things up out of the ground and guessing at how they may relate to individuals living in the present. The problem is, I would like to suggest as a geneticist, while the field of paleoanthropology, and the field of archaeology as well, give us certain insights into our past, possibilities about origins and journeys of the people alive today, they don't give us the probabilities about direct lines of descent that we really want . . . possibilities about our ancestry but not the probabilities that we're looking for as scientists.

We as geneticists take a slightly different approach. We start in the present and we work our back into the past. We take a genealogical approach. It's, in effect, like building a family tree . . . a family tree for everybody alive today. Now, genealogy is currently the second most popular hobby in the United States, after gardening and

I think it's poised to overtake gardening very soon. Now the problem is, everybody who's ever tried to construct a family tree eventually hits what we call a *brick wall* in the genealogical community—a point beyond which there is no written record. And beyond that point we simply enter this dark and mysterious realm we call history and ultimately, prehistory. But it turns out there is a written document in effect, that we're all carrying around inside of ourselves. In our DNA, inside of nearly every cell in our body, DNA that we've inherited from those parents, grandparents, great-grandparents, and so on, and this traces an unbroken line of descent going back in time. This is what allows us to trace back to the very earliest days of our species, allowing this global genealogical approach to the study of human history.

So by looking at people from all over the world, asking, in effect, a very open-ended scientific question: What is the pattern of human variation that we see today, globally? Looking in particular at two pieces of DNA that are proven to be incredibly valuable in the study of human origins and migrations. Mitochondrial DNA—mtDNA, which traces a purely maternal line of descent: Women pass it on to their children, everybody has it but only women pass it on. So if you have mitochondrial DNA, which everyone in the room does, you got it from your mom and she got it from her mom, and she got it from her mom. So it tells you about mother's, mother's, mother's, mother's mother, back to the very first mother.

There is an equivalent piece of DNA on the male side, in fact the chunk of DNA, the little chromosome as we call it, the Y-chromosome that makes men, men. But basically it traces a purely paternal line of descent, an unbroken line of descent going back in time. Sons inherit it from their fathers; they got it from their fathers, and so on—the Y-chromosome. By looking at the pattern of these genetic variants, these random changes that have occurred over time, on both of these lineages, we can construct family trees for everybody alive today.

It's a fascinating way of approaching the study of human history, because we, as people who study primarily modern human lineages, are getting only a glimpse of the actual process that went on to create that. So it's a huge addition to our understanding of the past.

Acknowledgments

62: Excerpt from "Why are Young, Educated Americans Going Back to the Farm" by Nelson Harvey, from Turnstyle/Youth Radio, September 21, 2011. Copyright © 2011 by Youth Radio. Reprinted by permission. **75:** Excerpt from "Love that Lingua Franca" by Diasann McLane from *National Geographic Traveler*, September, 2011. Reprinted by permission of the National Geographic Society. All rights reserved.

Sources

9: "Vikings Filed Their Teeth, Skeleton Study Shows," National Geographic News, February 3, 2006, **18:** "Last of the Cave People," *National Geographic*, February, 2012 **31:** "Ramses the Great," *National Geographic*, April, 1991, **40:** "Terra-Cotta Army Protects First Emperor's Tomb," NationalGeographic.com, **53:** "'Second Life,' Other Virtual Worlds Reshaping Human Interaction," National Geographic News, October 17, 2006, **84:** "Smarter Teams Are More Sensitive, Have More Women?" National Geographic News, September 30, 2010, **97:** "The Genographic Project," NationalGeographic.com, **106:** "Food: How Altered?" *National Geographic*, May, 2002.

Images

Inside front cover: William Allen/National Geogrpahic Stock, Kenneth Garrett/National Geographic Stock, Jeffrey Ufberg/WireImage Collection/Getty Images, Courtesy of Andrew Evans, Mark Thiessen/National Geographic Stock, **1:** Jill Schneider/National Geographic Stock, **2–3:** Kenneth Garrett/National Geographic Stock, **5:** Kenneth Garrett/National Geographic Stock, **6:** Tim Laman/National Geographic Stock, **6:** New York Public Library/Photo Researchers Collection/Getty Images, **9:** Staffan Hyll, **10:** Peter Essick/National Geographic Stock, **11:** Roy Toft/National Geographic Stock, **14:** James P. Blair/National Geographic Stock, **14:** James P. Blair/National Geographic Stock, **15:** Nicole Duplaix/Peter Arnold Collection/Getty Images, **15:** Frans Lanting/National Geographic Stock, **19:** Amy Toensing/National Geographic Stock, **20–21:** Annie Griffiths/National Geographic Stock, **21:** Annie Griffiths/National Geographic Stock, **23:** Kenneth Garrett/ National Geographic Stock, **24–25:** Kenneth Garrett/National Geographic Stock, **24:** Martin Gray/National Geographic Stock, **27:** Richard Nowitz/National Geographic Stock, **27:** Martin Gray/National Geographic Stock, **28:** Taylor S. Kennedy/National Geographic Stock, **28:** Kenneth Garrett/National Geographic Stock, **31:** O. Louis Mazzatenta/National Geographic Stock, **32:** O. Louis Mazzatenta/National Geographic Stock, **33:** Ira Block/National Geographic Stock, **36:** Raymond Gehman/National Geographic Stock, **36:** O.: Louis Mazzatenta/National Geographic Stock, **37:** O. Louis Mazzatenta/National Geographic Stock, **41:** O. Louis Mazzatenta/National Geographic Stock, **42–43:** Stephen Alvarez/National Geographic Stock, **43:** Kenneth Garrett/National Geographic Stock, **45:** Ola Dusegard/E+ Collection/Getty Images, **46:** Pete Mcbride/ National Geographic Stock, **47:** © creative soul - Fotolia.com, **49:** Richard Nowitz/National Geographic Stock, **50:** Klaus Vedfelt/Riser Collection/Getty Images, **50:** Asimetrica Juniper/Flickr Collection/Getty Images, **50:** © morganimation - Fotolia.com, **53:** The Washington Post/Getty Images, **54:** © Nmedia - Fotolia.com, **55:** Suzailan Shoroyo/National Geographic My Shot/National Geographic Stock, **58:** Derek Latta/E+ Collection/ Getty Images, **59:** Arthur Pollock/America 24-7 Collection/Getty Images, **59:** © Picture-Factory - Fotolia. com, **62:** Robert Kneschke/Shutterstock, **64–65:** Rob Lang/Taxi Collection/Getty Images, **65:** Jeffrey Ufberg/ WireImage Collection/Getty Images, **67:** Raul Touzon/National Geographic Stock, **68–69:** Raul Touzon/ National Geographic Stock, **71:** Flying Colours Ltd/Digital Vision Collection/Getty Images, **71:** © Jasmin Merdan - Fotolia.com, **72:** DAJ/Getty Images, **72:** Erik Dreyer/Stone Collection/Getty Images, **75:** PhotoTalk/ E+ Collection/Getty Images, **76:** © pink candy - Fotolia.com, **77:** Henrik Sorensen/Stone Collection/Getty Images, **80:** Lawrence Migdale/Photo Researchers Collection/Getty Images, **81:** © auremar - Fotolia.com, **81:** © auremar - Fotolia.com, **81:** © berc - Fotolia.com, **81:** Lane Oatey/Blue Jean Images/Getty Images, **84:** Marcin Balcerzak/Shutterstock, **86–87:** Beverly Joubert/National Geographic Stock, **87:** Beverly Joubert/ National Geographic Stock, **89:** Adrian Neal/Lifesize Collection/Getty Images, **90:** Ned M. Seidler/National Geographic Stock, **90–91:** © Gala_K - Fotolia.com, **93:** Ned M. Seidler/National Geographic Stock, **93:** David Sacks/Lifesize Collection/Getty Images, **94:** Pantheon / Superstock, **94:** Melissa Farlow/National Geographic Stock, **97:** © Mopic - Fotolia.com, **98:** Joe Stancampiano/National Geographic Stock, **99:** Jim Richardson/

National Geographic Stock, **102:** © Alexander Raths - Fotolia.com, **103:** © Chepko Danil - Fotolia.com, **103:** © Africa Studio - Fotolia.com, **103:** Floris Slooff/Shutterstock, **107:** Jim Richardson/National Geographic Stock, **108:** Sisse Brimberg/National Geographic Stock, **109:** Ngm Maps/National Geographic Stock